GOD, POWER, AND MAN

DR. SAFWAT BISHARA, DR. DALWAT BISHARA

authorHOUSE®

AuthorHouse™
1663 Liberty Drive
Bloomington, IN 47403
www.authorhouse.com
Phone: 1 (800) 839-8640

Published by AuthorHouse 03/22/2018

ISBN: 978-1-5462-3234-6 (sc)
ISBN: 978-1-5462-3232-2 (hc)
ISBN: 978-1-5462-3233-9 (e)

Library of Congress Control Number: 2018903626

Print information available on the last page.

King James Version (KJV)
Scriptures were taken from the King James Version of The Bible - Public Domain.

CONTENTS

DEDICATION

To men and women the world over

EPIGRAPH

"Every man has forgotten who he is. One may understand
the cosmos,
but never the ego; the self is more distant than any star.
Thou shalt love the
Lord thy God; but thou shalt not know thyself. We are all
under the same mental calamity; we have all forgotten our
names. We have forgotten what we really are."

G. K. Chesterton

"God is like the Sun; you can not look at it, but without
it you can not see
anything."

G. K. Chesterton

ACKNOWLEDGMENT

Thanks are due to Sarah Vaillancourt for editing this work. Her effort are greatly appreciated.

PREFACE

"In the beginning God created...." <u>GENESIS</u>, 1:1. "And God said, Let us make man in our image, after our likeness: and let them have dominion over the fish of the sea, and over the fowl of the air, and over the cattle, and over all the earth, and over every creeping thing that creepeth upon the earth. So God created man in his *own* image, in the image of God created he him; male and female created he them. And God blessed them, and God said unto them, Be fruitful, and multiply, and replenish the earth, and subdue it: and have dominion over the fish of the sea, and over the fowl of the air, and over every living thing that moveth upon the earth." <u>GENESIS</u>, 1: 26-28.

The Word of God makes it clear that God gave man dominion over all creatures: fish of the sea, fowl of the air, cattle, all the earth, and every creeping thing. The Bible conveys the heavenly intent of purpose by first telling it in verse 26 and then repeating the same command in verse 28.

Granted, not every man believes in creation. But whether man was created by God or is the end product of a random selection process, the fact remains that man is actually in control of his/her world.

The question is: How did man exercise his dominion over other creatures? Most significantly, how did man get along with other humans? Did man prove worthy of the power bestowed upon him by the Creator?

God aside, history is replete with stories of aggression, hostility, and betrayal.

GENESIS, 6: 5-12 says, "And God saw that the wickedness of man *was* great in the earth, and *that* every imagination of the thoughts of his heart *was* only evil continually. And it repented the Lord that he had made man on the earth, and it grieved him at his heart. And the Lord said, I will destroy man whom I have created from the face of the earth; both man, and beast, and the creeping thing, and the fowls of the air; for it repenteth me that I have made them. But Noah found grace in the eyes of the Lord. These are the generations of Noah: Noah was a just man and perfect in his generations, and Noah walked with God. And Noah begat three sons, Shem, Ham, and Ja-pheth. The earth also was corrupt before God, and the earth was filled with violence. And God looked upon the earth, and, behold, it was corrupt; for all flesh had corrupted his way upon the earth."

At the fullness of time our Lord Jesus Christ took the form of a man and lived among us—a sinless life that brought salvation to those who believe in Him.

But not everyone did.

The Apostle Paul writes, "As it is written, There is none righteous, no, not one: There is none that understandeth, there is none that seeketh after God. They are all gone out of the way, they are together become unprofitable; there is none that doeth good, no, not one." ROMANS 3, 10-12.

In ROMANS 7, 18-19, the Apostle goes from the general to the specific as he states, "For I know that in me (that is, in my flesh,) dwelleth no good thing: for to will is present with me; but *how* to perform that which is good I find not. For the good that I would I do not: but the evil which I would not, that I do."

Not much has changed ever since.

We tend to think of Adolph Hitler and Joseph Stalin as if they were uniquely evil persons, but the truth is everyone on the planet would have done the same if they believed their philosophies and were not accountable to anybody. Many a dictator forgets that the purpose of the state is not to govern the individual but to protect him/her. <u>AGENDA 2</u>, <u>MASTERS OF DECEIT</u>, Agenda documentary.com, DVD.

On a different scale, Robert Clark, <u>THE ECONOMIST</u>, November 2, 2013, p. 21, offers a suggestion on how to deal with present-day politicians. He proposes "creating the Large Ego Collider in which our congressmen are accelerated into ever higher-energy collisions with their oppositely charged colleagues. The goal is mutual annihilation and the creation of a new particle, the theorized but hitherto unobserved Electable Moderate Centrist."

The aggression of man is boundless. No wonder about "one-sixth of the earth's land surface is protected in one way or another." <u>THE ECONOMIST</u>, October 26, 2013, p. 50. This contrasts with marine reserves that, at most, cover three percent. The American-based Pew Charitable Trusts are proposing to "designate the Exclusive Economic Zone around the Pitcarin islands in the South Pacific as a marine protected area." This would ban fishing "in 830,000 square kilometers (320,000 square miles) of sea around Pitcarin." The island makes a perfect choice; it is scarcely populated (65 people) and quite removed from other areas—4,800 kilometers east of New Zealand and 6,000 kilometers west of Ecuador. The hope is that these precautions are enough to keep man away.

Man realizes that he has to protect marine life from man. Laws, law enforcement, and courts protect man from man. The Word of God seeks to protect man from *himself.*

And the Creator has designed physical protection for the newborn. An article in <u>THE ECONOMIST</u>, October 26, 2013, p. 91, reports on research that identified a protein in mothers' milk that protects infants against the dreadful HIV infection.

It has long been known that mothers' milk has all nutrients necessary for the baby. Many believe that it also has vaccines against illnesses the weak body is yet unable to handle. What has recently been proved is that mothers' milk has some proteins that "suppress the HIV virus's reproduction."

Researchers at Duke University in North Carolina have found that a single protein called "tenascin-C... disables HIV by locking onto a protein on the virus's surface." It was observed that only ten percent of HIV-infected mothers did transmit the virus to infants through suckling. This could be explained by the fact that tenascin-C in mothers' milk is as effective at locking the HIV virus as "antibodies generated by the immune system for that specific purpose."

THE ECONOMIST'S article claims that it is "a complete coincidence" that tenascin-C has "the right shape to attach itself to HIV's envelope protein." It goes on to say "because AIDS is such a recent disease that evolution could not have had time to throw up a novel anti-HIV protein of this sort," then it seems to be "a complete coincidence" that tenascin-C has "the right shape to attach itself to HIV's envelope protein."

Is it really a coincidence that two proteins happen to have the right molecular structure with oppositely-charged atoms coming together to bring about the forces of attachment? Or it is the Creator's design to provide protection for those who can not defend themselves? Is AIDS a recent disease or did people die from it a long time ago but no one then knew why?

Whenever evolutionists are confronted with new scientific facts, they usually claim *coincidence*.

God created man and gave him dominion over creatures of the air, in the sea, and on land. The Creator sent prophets to assuage man's inclination towards sin. When all this failed, He sent His only begotten Son. For three years He lived a sinless life, and performed all miracles even raising the dead—not one but three different persons. Yes, He came to be the sacrificial lamb. His crucifixion and resurrection offer hope for an otherwise doomed human race.

How and what man did with the power entrusted him is the subject of this book.

PART I

PART I: POWER OF RELIGION

One might think of God at the top of a triangle, where power and man form the base. But when God is left out, power changes into tyranny. History, old and recent, is replete with instances of good (constructive) power as well as abusive power.

The *I AM* has always been, is, and will ever be on His throne. His love for humanity is on display everywhere since the creation. But man's response to the Creator has not always been in kind.

In it all, God never lost hope in His creation. He sent prophets to help man get back in touch with his Creator. When all failed, He sent His only begotten Son. He was crucified by man. His ascension to heaven is man's hope for an eternal life. The Lord Jesus Christ reconciled the sinful man to a holy God.

CHAPTER 1

IN CHRISTIANITY

JOHN 3:16 says, "For God so loved the world, that he gave his only begotten Son, that whosoever believeth in him should not perish, but have everlasting life."

God cared about man's life on earth and beyond. Who is more qualified than a medical doctor to describe the miracle of the human body?

Dr. Richard A. Swenson, MORE THAN MEETS THE EYE, Navpress, Colorado Springs, Colorado, 2000, writes, "When God set out to create humanity He put His genius on display.... As a scientist with training in both medicine and physics, it is easily apparent to me that the majesty of God is revealed in the human body. His fingerprints are, in fact, all over us."

Swenson, M.D., lists some figures about the human body.

"There are forty-two thousand fewer neurons in the right side of your brain than the left side."

At any given moment, one has "18.755 billion trillion air molecules" in his/her lungs.

"Ninety percent of our atoms are replaced annually. Every five years, one hundred percent of our atoms turn over and become new atoms," isotope studies reveal.

The human body contains 10 to the power 28 atoms (1 followed by 28 zeros), according to David M. Baughan, M.D., <u>CONTEMPORARY SCIENTIFIC PRINCIPLES AND FAMILY MEDICINE</u>, Volume 19, January/February 1987, p. 42.

The details are staggering. The human brain is a three-pound organ but it is "the most complex and orderly arrangement of matter in the universe." Isaac Asimov, <u>IN THE GAME OF ENERGY AND THERMODYNAMICS YOU CAN'T EVEN BREAK EVEN</u>, Smithsonian Journal, June 1970, p. 10.

The human brain has ten (some say a hundred) billion neurons. "Each neuron is... in contact with ten thousand other neurons for a total of 100 trillion neurological interconnections," writes Dr. Swenson.

The brain has the capacity to hold "information equivalent to that contained in twenty-five million books."

Within the neuron (brain cell), "the signal is electrical. But where one nerve connects with its neighbor, in a connection called a synapse, the signal switches into a chemical message... ferried across the synapse by a neurotransmitter." Dopamine is one example of one hundred different neurotransmitters. "The electrical activity of the brain... generates current running down the neurons... [and] is responsible for brain waves."

The most sophisticated organ of the miraculous human body is in the head. No wonder the word of God says, God is the head of the Church.

After the invention of the computer, some used the simile that the brain is like a computer. Now, "one group of scientists... wish to make computers more like brains." <u>THE ECONOMIST</u>, August 3, 2013, pp. 67-69. The goal is to design a computer "that has some—and preferably all—of three characteristics that brains have and computers do not. These are: low power consumption,... fault tolerance,... a lack of need to be programmed."

Human brains use about 20 watts as opposed to the megawatts used by supercomputers "currently used to try to simulate them." Human brains "lose neurons all the time," but the loss of one transistor "can wreck a microprocessor." The most challenging feature is the need for computers to be programmed to follow "the fixed paths and branches of a predetermined algorithm." Our brains "learn and change spontaneously as they interact with the world."

A federation of European scientific institutions is working to build a simulacrum of the brain by 2023 under the auspices of the Human Brain Project with a budget of $1.3 billion. "America's equivalent of the neuromorphic part of the Human Brain Project, the Systems of Neuromorphic Adaptive Plastic Scalable Electronics, SYNAPSE, [is] paid for by the Defense Advanced Research Projects Agency."

Truly the greatest challenge for the neuromorphic engineers would be to invent brain-like machines that need not be programmed, but "learn and change spontaneously as they interact with the world." More challenging though is to mimic the human brain's ability to "create" music, a novel, a scientific theory, or even a child's toy.

The great composer Johann Sebastian Bach stands shoulder to shoulder with "Monteverdi, Beethoven, and Mozart [who] have achieved greatness in various ways, but it is Bach... who gives us the voice of God—in human form." THE ECONOMIST, October 12, 2013, p. 96. Bach's ultimate goal... "was to compose a well-regulated or orderly church music to the glory of God."

In his book BACH: MUSIC IN THE CASTLE OF HEAVEN, Sir John Eliot Gardiner "discovers a wealth of hitherto unseen invention and ingenuity... it comes down to an act of faith."

Once at Thomaskirche, Bach "started on a bout of furious cantana-composing... for three years he came up with a new one—about 20 minutes' worth of music—for the church service every Sunday. During that time he also produced full-length Passions for each Easter... [he] left a lasting legacy."

Bach died in 1750.

A robot can surely respond to a command, but can it compose a piece of music? Write a poem? Or is there a divine "component" of the human brain other than transistors, watts, and algorithms put together in a machine? Can the created match the Creator?

THE ATLANTIC, May 2016, pp. 36-38, reports on the greatest poet alive. Leslie Allan Murray can "read more than twenty languages, and lift the back of a motor car by hand," quotes his biographer Peter Alexander. James Parker writes that Murray is "our greatest living English-language poet."

Murray was "born into rural squalor in New South Wales, Australia, in 1938. Holes in the walls, cocking over the fire, no running water, no electricity. His father tended cows and hacked timber,... Les was often barefoot." He lost his mother at the age of 12. In high school he was "skillfully and pitilessly victimized." Murray moved to Sydney to attend college where, for a short time, he befriended aesthetes and protohippies. This left him "with a Chestertonian horror of selfish bohemians, moral chaos, ideologies that look like life styles, and the like." In his twenties he converted to Catholicism and wrote more than three dozen books most of them dedicated to "the glory of God."

As it is usually the case, the media caricatured Les Murray as an "anti modern stodge." He is now 78, and he has not stopped writing.

Nothing is wrong with man's ambition to mimic the human brain, but maybe we should keep our hopes in check. Ignoring God's power and the mystery of creation would open us up to a disappointing awakening.

Some choose to replace luck for God's power and intervention. Robert H. Frank writes, "I have discovered that chance plays a far larger role in life outcomes than most people realize." THE ATLANTIC, May 2016, pp. 19-21. Frank cites the circumstances that led Michael Lewis to write his "1989 best seller, LIAR'S POKER, which described how Wall Street financial maneuvering was transforming the world."

Addressing the 2012 graduating class of Princeton University, Michael Lewis described the "series of chance events that helped make him... a celebrated author." Invited to a dinner, Lewis was seated next to the wife of an executive at Solomon Brothers. "She more or less forced her husband to give me a job. I knew next to nothing about Solomon Brothers." Lewis was assigned the "very best job in the place to observe the growing madness. They turned me into the house derivatives expert." He found it quite lucky to sit "next to that Solomon Brothers lady."

Here a question springs to mind. Was it luck that had Michael Lewis seated next to the wife of an executive at a major investment bank? No one can definitely exclude coincidence, but an equally possible explanation is God's planning. By the same token, it is impossible to prove that divine intervention was behind the outcome that led Michael Lewis to write his 1989 best seller.

"People really don't like to hear success explained away as luck—especially successful people," writes Lewis. Similarly, many don't feel satisfied to explain away their success as simply part of God's plan.

Rebellion against the Creator comes naturally to man—since Adam and Eve. It takes *humility* to give credit to the One who is due.

Almost simultaneously to Robert H. Frank's article, THE ATLANTIC, April 2016, had a three-page article (pp. 22-24) about having a sense of purpose as the source of an "individual's job satisfaction."

> Copenhagen's Happiness Research Institute surveyed 2,600 Danish workers, from every sector and type of job, about the source of professional contentment. The winner, by a sizable margin, was a sense of purpose, which contributed twice as much to an individual's job satisfaction as did the runner-up, having a high-quality manager.

It has been claimed that the need for a sense of purpose grows at midlife. Eric H. Erikson, the developmental psychologist, observes that "at some point in middle age a person begins to shift from investing inward—building a career, raising a family, buying a house, accumulating wealth and prestige—to investing outward."

Barbara Bradley Hagerty points to copious research that indicated that a sense of purpose is a good indicator of "mental and physical robustness."

> Compared with people who feel little purpose in life, those who report a strong sense of purpose... are far less likely to suffer a stroke or a heart attack, and are less susceptible to viruses... diabetes, metastatic cancer, and neurodegenerative disease.

Evidence as well as logic seem to support the idea of having a "sense of purpose" as the impetus behind a meaningful, satisfying life. It helps to keep the mind focused and the soul gratified as the days go by and the fruits of one's efforts start to be felt.

Barbara Hagerty quotes Philip A. Pizzo, the director of Stanford's program, the Distinguished Careers Institute, as saying, "When people get to their mid-career phase... [they] become anxious and just start doing things that are not connected or not meaningful... just to feel like they are contributing."

Without a compass man can easily lose sight of the way. Wrong decisions can be costly, but the Word of God is a "lamp onto my feet." In the Christian economy God has a plan for every human being. Our responsibility is just to have a submissive spirit willing to obey the Holy Spirit as He whispers the Creator's will.

One of the greatest Christian apologists of recent times is C.S. Lewis.

George M. Marsden writes, "He points people to see, as he has, the time-tested beauty of God's love in Jesus Christ. Not everyone will see the beauty or be persuaded. But those who get a true glimpse will be drawn in by its power." THE WALL STREET JOURNAL, March 25, 2016, p. A9.

One of Lewis's books that has gathered great interest is <u>MERE CHRISTIANITY</u> with "more than 3.5 million copies [sold] in English. It has been translated into at least 36 languages and... the book that, next to the Bible, educated Chinese Christians are most likely to have read."

Marsden's article describes how <u>MERE CHRISTIANITY</u> evolved from being "four sets of BBC radio talks on basic Christianity," presented by Lewis during "the dark days of World War II," until 1952 when he collected them together under the new title.

It is under tough times that most of us turn to God seeking His face. We tend to forget that His love to mankind is always there; our response makes the difference.

The fact is that the perception of God, and how to approach His will, differentiate Christianity from all other religions.

Over two billion Christians worldwide believe in a loving, forgiving God, and there are 1.3 billion Muslims who believe in a God "who is aloof, vengeful, punishing whom He pleases and rewarding those whom He desires to favor." Safwat Bishara. <u>TWO DIFFERENT RELIGIONS. HOW ISLAM PERCEIVES CHRISTIANITY AND WHAT IS THE TRUTH</u>, Authorhouse, Bloomington, Indiana, 2013, 274 pages.

To get favor with God all able-bodied Muslims are required to perform the *haj*, "a trek to Islam's holiest site[s] in Saudi Arabia." <u>THE ECONOMIST</u>, October 12, 2013, p. 74. A Muslim needs to do the *haj* at least once in a lifetime—it is one of the five pillars of the faith. This applies to Sunni as well as Shia Muslims.

Shia Muslims do not go to Saudi Arabia but go in huge numbers to visit shrines in Iraq. Abundant tumult there is less likely to deter those traveling for religious reasons than ordinary citizens. Shia pilgrims go to Karbala and Najaf in Iraq "despite the threat of bombs" by Sunni Muslims. *Ibid.*

Although religious tourism has slowed down considerably, the *haj* has "both expanded and gone upmarket. Oil wealth and a rising identification with Islam have made it a huge moneymaker. Posh hotel chains have piled into Mecca, Saudi Arabia." *Ibid.*

Such is the motive to get favor with God. The average Muslims—even those who can not afford the *haj* expenses—save for years to fulfill this obligation. The next chapter will deal more with the power of Islamic religion.

The purity and beauty of Christianity could not always stand in the face of Satan. After he failed to tempt our Lord Jesus Christ on the mountain, he set his eyes on Christ's bride—the Church. He has been bent on fighting the Word of God by deception and every possible means he could muster including "misrepresent[ing] the character of God, to cause men to cherish a false conception of the Creator, and thus regard Him with fear and hate rather than with love." Ellen G. White, <u>COSMIC CONFLICT. GOOD AND EVIL WAGE WAR FOR PLANET EARTH</u>, Review and Herald Publishing Association, Washington, D.C., 1982, 640 pages.

The war between good and evil has been on the rise over time since creation and is likely to intensify and continue until the end of time.

"When the apostles of Christ were to bear His gospel to the world... they were especially endowed with the enlightenment of the Spirit. But as the Church approaches her final deliverance, Satan is to work with greater power." *Ibid., 13.*

Satan has been in continuous pursuit of "those who dare to resist his deceptions." His persecution may be "traced in the history of patriarchs, prophets, and apostles, of martyrs and reformers." *Ibid., 14.*

Fearing the spread of Christianity, paganism kindled the "fires of persecution." Christians were "stripped of their possessions and driven from their homes." Many Christians "sealed their testimony with their blood." *Ibid., 38.*

Persecution started about the time of Paul's martyrdom and "continued with greater or lesser fury for centuries." *Ibid., 39.*

Christians were accused of rebellion against the empire and endured "popular hatred and suspicion." Many were thrown to the lions, others were burned alive. Punishment was public, and "often made the chief entertainment" in amphitheaters.

> Beneath the hills outside the city of Rome, long galleries had been tunneled through earth and rock; the dark and intricate network of passages extended for miles beyond the city walls. In these underground retreats the followers of Christ buried their dead.

As has always been the case over two millennia, persecution of Christians strengthened rather than weakened the Church. Satan and the spirit of the Antichrist failed to destroy the faith by violence.

Satan therefore planted "his banner in the Christian church." *Ibid., 40.* If he could deceive the followers of Christ into displeasing God "they would fall an easy prey." And the plan worked well—then and now.

By Satan's deceiving powers some within the Church started on the path of idolizing "allurements of temporal prosperity and worldly honor." *Ibid., 41.* People lost the sense and conviction of sin and instead called it a "mistake." And removing sin from the conscience of man meant no need for repentance or a change of heart.

The great adversary made inroads in the Church. A state of fearful peril ensued among the faithful followers of Christ.

Some Christians declared that

> they could make no compromise. Others were in favor of yielding or modifying some features of their faith and uniting with those who had accepted a part of Christianity.... Under a cloak of pretended Christianity, Satan was ingratiating himself into the Church. *Ibid.*

9

But was Satan the sole culprit? He plays with our minds, and it is up to us whether to listen or not. The adversary plants the seed of deceit, but man has the power to resist if he so chooses.

The struggle between those who stood firm in their belief and the compromisers continued until "most of the Christians... consented to lower their standard, and a union was formed between Christianity and paganism." *Ibid.*

The result was some "Unsound doctrines... idolatrous ceremonies" being incorporated into the faith. Christianity became "corrupted, and the church lost her purity and power." *Ibid.*

There can never be a union between the "Prince of Light and the Prince of Darkness, and there can be no union between their followers." *Ibid., 42.*

The conflict resumed. The faithful followers of Christ "decided to dissolve all union with the apostate church." *Ibid., 43.* Though few in numbers, not wealthy, with no honorary titles, they were "a terror to evildoers." *Ibid., 44.* Not surprisingly, they were "hated by the wicked... who sought to throw off the restraint of the holy Spirit [and] put to death God's people."

To differ with other people is one thing, but to put to death those whom we differ with is another. Even with highly emotional subjects, such as religion, such brutality is defenseless. But man can always explain away his deeds under the pretense of defending the "true" faith. Without the restraint of the Holy Spirit, evil sneaks in its head as it has always done even as "Abel was hated by the ungodly Cain."

But the Lord Jesus Christ foresaw the "doubts that would press upon [the disciples'] souls in days of trial and darkness." <u>JOHN</u> 15:20 says "If they persecuted me, they will also persecute you."

Since the early days of Christianity persecution was a hallmark of its history. The "furnace of affliction" endured by the early followers of Christ helped them get purified, and their "consistent course [helped] condemn the ungodly and unbelieving." *Ibid., 45.*

Early in the fourth century Constantine, the emperor of Rome, converted to Christianity. One form of persecution was put on hold but his conversion brought to the church "the world cloaked with a form of righteousness." *Ibid., 47.*

Gradually, at first in silence, then openly as it gained strength, the "mystery of inequity carried forward its deceptive and blasphemous work." *Ibid.*

So as persecution halted and Christianity got into palaces of kings, the church opted for the pomp and pride of the world instead of the humble simplicity of the Lord and His apostles.

Corruption progressed. The compromise between paganism and Christianity led to the "development of the man of sin" prophesied in the Word of God.

Satan tried to form a compromise with Christ but the Lord rebuked him and "forced him to depart." The great deceiver was more successful with man. The church started to seek the "favor and support of the great men of earth." Having rejected Christ, the church was well positioned to "yield allegiance to the representative of Satan—the bishop of Rome." *Ibid., 48.*

The Pope, the head of the church, had full authority over bishops and pastors all over the world. Furthermore, he had been declared infallible and demanded the homage of all.

As the saying goes, power corrupts and absolute power corrupts absolutely. To establish the papal authority, it was deemed necessary to keep people ignorant of the Scriptures.

> The Bible exalts God and places finite men in their true position; therefore its sacred truths must be concealed and suppressed. This logic was adopted by the Roman Church.

11

For hundreds of years the circulation of the Bible was prohibited. The people were forbidden to read it or to have it in their houses, and unprincipled priests and prelates interpreted its teachings to sustain their pretensions.... Thus the *Pope* came to be... endowed with authority over church and state. *Ibid., 49.*

An era of spiritual darkness set in. The Bible unavailable, people were ignorant of the Scriptures, and only priests and prelates had access to and interpretation of the Word. With no accountability except to the pope, who had no accountability except to God, the stage was set for the arch deceiver to complete his work. "He was resolved to gather the Christian world under his banner and to exercise his power through his vicegerent, the proud pontiff who claimed to be the representative of Christ." *Ibid., 50.*

The job of the great apostate was made easier as he had to focus his attacks on just one person.

The Papacy continued to grow stronger until it became firmly established in the sixth century. The bishop of Rome was "declared to be the head over the entire church. Paganism had given place to the papacy." *Ibid., 51.*

For twelve centuries the papal oppression continued.

"Christians were forced to choose either to yield their integrity and accept the papal... worship, or to... suffer death by the rack, the fagot, or the headsman's ax." *Ibid.* The establishment of the powerful Roman Church was the beginning of the Dark Ages.

Instead of faith in Christ, it was the Pope of Rome who was worshiped. People looked to the Pope who delegated his authority to the priests. They taught worshipers that reaching God was possible only through their earthly mediator. No personal relationship could be established between a Christian and the Lord Jesus Christ.

Because the Pope was the only mediator between God and man, he should be obeyed. "A deviation from his requirements was sufficient cause for the severest punishment to be visited upon the bodies and souls of the offenders." *Ibid., 52.*

Allow man absolute authority and power, and over time chances are he will be the abuser. Born with the inherited sin from Adam, only God's Holy Spirit can restrain the erring and cruelty of man. Suppress the Scriptures and "man comes to regard himself as supreme."

About the end of the eighth century the church claimed that the bishops of Rome had the same spiritual power that the church leaders possessed in the first ages of the Christian faith. To support this claim, "Ancient writings were forged by monks. Decrees of councils before unheard of were discovered." *Ibid., 53.*

In the eleventh century Pope Gregory VII took further steps toward perfecting the dominance of the Roman Church. He claimed the "power to depose emperors, and... that no sentence which he pronounced could be reversed by anyone, but that it was his prerogative to reverse the decisions of all others." *Ibid., 54.*

The progression of Rome's absolute power reached the apex. The Pope, in effect, controlled the spiritual as well as the political destiny of all believers.

When the German Emperor Henry IV appeared to be disregarding the Pope's authority, he was ex-communicated and dethroned. The monarch was terrified by the threats of his own princes who saw an opportunity to rebel against him pursuant to the Pope's mandate.

Interestingly, man can hardly miss an opportunity to make further gains. The emperor's princes chose their own self interest rather than standing beside what was right.

Henry felt pressure to make amends with Rome. In midwinter, the emperor took his wife on a trip across the Alps. Upon reaching the castle where Pope Gregory had withdrawn, he was allowed in an outer court where he spent three days fasting and making confessions. It was then that the pontiff "condescended to grant him pardon." *Ibid.*

13

Such was the power of the Pope. The German emperor was made an example for others who would contemplate challenging Rome's authority.

Elated, Gregory boasted that it was "his duty to pull down the pride of kings." *Ibid.*

Is there a limit that quenches man's appetite for power, authority, fame, money,... etc? Only the Holy Spirit can muster that; our responsibility is to listen to his whispers. The Holy Spirit does not force man to obey but softly speaks to his conscience.

The war between good and evil overwhelms humanity to reach the person who is titled the "representative of God on earth." *Ibid.*

With greater power Rome put forth an increasing number of erroneous doctrines.

> Remission of sins, past, present, and future, and release from all pains... were promised to all who would enlist in the pontiff's wars to extend his temporal dominion,... or to exterminate those who dared deny his spiritual supremacy.... Payment of money to the Church... might free people from sin. *Ibid., 55.*

In the thirteenth century the Inquisition was established. "The mangled forms of millions of martyrs cried to God for vengeance upon that apostate power." *Ibid., 56.* Everyone, including kings and emperors, obeyed the decrees coming out of Rome. Peoples' destinies before and after death appeared to be under the pontiff's control.

In effect the Pope became the spiritual *and* political authority.

With the Scriptures almost unknown to the people as well as to the priests, the papal leaders "exercised power without limit, and practiced vice without restraint." *Ibid.*

In such a social and spiritual environment it is no wonder that Europe had made no progress in the arts, architecture, or culture. Every trend has its origins: the moral and intellectual paralysis that had fallen upon the continent was the outcome.

But all this gloom could not distinguish the light of the truth. Witnesses for God stood firm in their belief. Rome branded them as heretics. Their writings were "suppressed, misrepresented, or mutilated." *Ibid., 58.*

Few traces of the existence of these men of God could be found. Rome sought to destroy everything she deemed heretical, whether it be persons or writings.

Scattered spots of light carried the day for Christendom.

The United Kingdom, geographically distant from Rome, and separated by sea from the continent, kept the gospel from the early centuries uncorrupted by "Romish apostasy." *Ibid., 59.* But still persecution of the first churches in Britain was Rome's gift. Many fled persecution in England to Scotland and then to Ireland.

After the heathen Saxons invaded Britain, the Christians retreated to the mountains. But the *light* continued to shine. From Ireland, Columba and collaborators went to the island of Iona where a school was established and from which missionaries went to Scotland, England, Germany, Switzerland, and even Italy.

But Rome was relentless in subduing the primitive Christians in Britain. The emissary of Rome demanded that these Christian churches acknowledge the supremacy of the sovereign pontiff. Refusal to comply with the Pope's demand brought threats of war.

The religion that was spread only by love and peace then had its leader threatening war against anyone who opposed him.

Such was the coercion exerted by the head of the church in Rome.

How far his approach was from Christ's message of love and forgiveness. The disciples spread the faith by peace and preaching Christ's message of a loving Father who cherished everyone who came to his senses and accepted the redeeming blood of the Savior.

Christianity has always been a message of choice. God created man and bestowed upon him the freedom of deciding for himself.

As noted earlier, there can never be unity between good and evil. Separation of the true church from that of Rome ensued.

One of the main reasons behind the separation was the hatred between the church of Rome and the church of Christ. Darkness could not bear the light that exposed its evil thoughts and deeds.

> Satan had urged on the papal priests and prelates to bury the word of truth beneath the rubbish of error, heresy, and superstition; but... it was preserved uncorrupted through all the ages of darkness. It bore not the stamp of man, but the impress of God. *Ibid., 64.*

The arch deceiver inspired but it is *man* who responded.

Many Christians did not succumb to the claims of Rome. They knew that the mediation of men between God and sinners is in vain. Christ is the only mediator. His blood is the ultimate sacrifice paid to redeem man. Confession of sins goes directly to Him, and He alone can forgive.

The Waldensian missionaries worked relentlessly to spread the true faith. "With naked feet and in garments coarse and travel-stained as were those of their Master, they passed through great cities and penetrated to distant lands." *Ibid., 67.* They joyfully sacrificed the comforts of life, and their blood witnessed for the truth.

Rome was not happy.

The faith of the ancient church was testimony to Rome's apostasy. Bitter hatred and persecution was not unexpected.

As these missionaries refused to surrender the Scriptures, Rome sought to "blot them from the earth." *Ibid., 70.*

Inquisitors began targeting God's people at their mountain homes in the most terrible crusade in church history. Their dwellings and chapels were destroyed.

The taste of blood fed the beast into more killings.

"No charge could be brought against the moral character of this proscribed class.... Their grand offense was that they would not worship God according to the will of the Pope." *Ibid., 71.* They then deserved every insult and torture invented by man.

The Pope issued an official decree condemning the missionaries as heretics to be slaughtered.

To encourage members of the church to participate in such cruelty the decree legitimized their "title to any property they might have illegally acquired." *Ibid.* It promised forgiveness of all sins even the killing of a heretic.

The Waldenses preached God's word centuries before Martin Luther was born. They planted seeds of the Reformation that "began in the time of Wycliffe, [and] grew broad and deep in the days of Luther." *Ibid., 72.*

How sad it is to recall the atrocities committed by *man* against man in the context of "defending" the most peaceful message of the Gospels.

John Wycliffe, the herald of reform, lived in England in the fourteenth century.

He strongly opposed the abuses set forth by the authority of Rome. As chaplain for the king he fought against payment of tribute to the Pope from the English monarch. As a professor of theology at Oxford University, Wycliffe was at the right place to preach God's word to the future leaders of England.

But his outstanding contribution to Christendom was the translation of the Scriptures into the English language. He made the word of God available to the people of England and thus deprived Rome of one of its strong weapons intently used for centuries.

Because printing was not yet known, the availability of the Bible was both a slow and a tedious process. "Wycliffe now taught the distinctive doctrines of Protestantism—salvation through faith in Christ, and the sole infallibility of the Scriptures." *Ibid., 81.*

Three times Wycliffe was brought to trial, but he did not retract and fearlessly defended his teachings.

Rome summoned Wycliffe for trial before the papal tribunal which had frequently ordered the killing of saints. An attack of palsy prevented him from going to Rome. He wrote a letter that was a rebuke to the "pomp and pride of the papal see." *Ibid., 83.*

One day just before he was getting ready to dispense communion in his church, palsy attacked him again, and he died shortly afterward.

God protected Wycliffe from Rome until he was able to lay a foundation for the great movement of the Reformation.

> Instead of the church speaking through the Pope, he declared the only true authority to be the voice of God speaking through His word.... Thus he turned the minds of men from the Pope and the Church of Rome to the word of God. *Ibid., 85.*

Not surprisingly, Rome was unhappy. The hatred of the papists could not be satisfied except after his bones were exhumed and publicly burned.

The doctrines that Wycliffe taught continued to spread and the "pitiless storm of persecution burst upon those who had dared to accept the Bible as their guide." *Ibid., 86.*

The English kings sacrificed the Reformers in order to appease Rome. Martyrdom of the advocates of truth was not uncommon.

Here a question springs to mind. Who or what is to blame for such cruelty?

Can we blame Christianity? The answer is definitely negative. The teachings of our Lord Jesus Christ call for love and forgiveness. People flock to the faith out of conviction—coercion, implicit or explicit, never existed. But *man* is the ultimate distorter of the truth to fit his worldly desires and ambitions.

On the European continent Bohemia had the Bible planted in the ninth century.

It was translated, and public worship was conducted in the language of its people. But as the power of Rome intensified, that situation could not be ignored.

Pope Gregory VII issued a bull forbidding public worship in the Bohemian tongue. In this respect Christianity resembled Islam which forbids the translation of the Qur'an into any language other than Arabic.

John Huss, orphaned by the death of his father early in life, had a pious mother who "sought to secure this heritage for her son." *Ibid., 89.*

Huss was a sincere adherent of the Roman Church. After graduating from the University of Prague, he entered the priesthood. Within a short period he joined the court of the king, became a professor then rector of the university where he was educated.

Jerome was a citizen of Prague. When he returned from England, he brought the writings of Wycliffe with him. Huss read the doctrines with great interest.

News of the work arrived in Rome.

"Huss was soon summoned to appear before the Pope." *Ibid., 91.*

He knew that going to Rome meant certain death.

When he refused to obey the order, the Pope declared Prague to be excluded from offices and privileges. The sentence caused immense alarm as it came from the Pope—the representative of God himself—who held the keys of heaven and hell, and had the power to "invoke temporal as well as spiritual judgments."

Instead of Huss laboring alone, Jerome joined in the work of reform. Jerome was a genius and eloquent, and Huss possessed strength of character. Their united efforts helped extend the reform more rapidly.

In Rome, three Popes were fighting for the papacy. Their battle brought crime and tumult among many Christians. Each Pope encouraged his group to buy arms and recruit soldiers. To achieve this goal money must be raised. So "offices and blessings of the church were offered for sale." *Ibid., 93.*

A house built on sand can not withstand the storm when it comes.

To address the chaos that was engulfing Europe, a council was summoned to Constance in Germany. The goal was to "heal the schism in the church and to root out heresy." Ibid., 94.

The two anti-Popes were summoned to appear before the council, as was John Huss.

Before appearing before the council, Huss had obtained a "safe-conduct from the king of Bohemia, and received one also from the Emperor Sigismund."

When he arrived in Constance, the emperor's safe-conduct was extended to include personal assurance of protection by the Pope.

But these declarations were violated and the reformer was soon arrested on orders of the Pope and cardinals. Huss was kept prisoner in a strong castle.

When a low-level criminal makes a promise that he later disavows, people may not be totally surprised since he is, after all, a criminal. But when the leader of the Church of Rome—God's supposed representative on earth—goes back on his word, something is terribly wrong with *man* even he happens to be the Pope.

In chains, Huss was finally brought before the council. After a long trial he was given the choice between recanting his doctrines or suffering death. He chose the latter.

Sadly, Huss's options offered by the church were more restrictive than the options offered Christians by the invading armies of Islam (Chapter 2). Muslims offered Christians the options of paying "gizya" (high taxes), or recanting Christianity, or death. One is tempted to say that Huss faced more cruel condemnation by the papal authorities than did Christians under the control of Islamic armies.

The secular authorities led Huss away to be executed. He was fastened to the stake, and when "the flames kindled about him, he began to sing." *Ibid., 99.*

Rome felt satisfied.

But Huss's execution showed the world the cruelty of the papacy.

> The execution of Huss had kindled a flame of indignation and horror in Bohemia. It was felt by the whole nation that he had fallen prey to the malice of the priests and treachery of the emperor. *Ibid., 104.*

When Jerome heard about the reformer's imprisonment, he set out for Constance. He soon realized that there was nothing he could do to deliver Huss and tried to flee the city but was arrested.

After one year in prison, the council decided against burning Jerome to avoid the indignation brought about by violating Huss's safe-conduct. Instead they planned to force Jerome to retract his doctrines. His refusal brought a sentence of condemnation, and he gave his life at the same spot where Huss did before him.

In Bohemia strife and bloodshed continued.

Faithful Christians suffered a bloody persecution. They formed a distinct church and called themselves "United Brethren'" Messengers secretly sent out to different countries made the Brethren aware of isolated spots of true believers who were also objects of persecution.

A correspondence began with the Waldensian Christians.

By the end of the fifteenth century, there was a slow but sure increase in the number of churches of the Brethren.

At the right time God's providence and mercy called for Martin Luther to stand firm in leading the church from the "darkness of popery into the light of a purer faith... through him God accomplished a great work for the reformation of the church and the enlightenment of the world." *Ibid., 108.*

Growing up, Luther endured hardship, privation, and tough discipline.

He entered a monastery and became a monk. His perception of God was a stern, cruel, and tyrannical judge (not much different from the Muslims' perception of God).

But the Creator had bestowed on Luther a "retentive memory, a lively imagination, strong reasoning powers... [that] soon placed him in the foremost rank among his associates." *Ibid., 109.* He was ordained a priest and appointed a professor at Wittenberg University.

God led Luther to visit Rome.

There he saw that inequity was rampant among all classes of the clergy. Early in life he was loyal to the Roman Church. But his trip to Rome made such an impression on him that he eventually severed all connections with the church in Rome.

Luther made it known that Christians should get only those doctrines based on the sacred Scriptures. These words were in direct conflict with papal supremacy and essentially established "the vital principle of the Reformation." *Ibid., 113.*

To erect St. Peter's Church in Rome, considerable sums of money had to be raised. By authority of the Pope "indulgences for sin" were publicly offered. It was not hard to deceive the people since the Bible had been purposefully withheld from them. "Certificates of Pardon" promised the purchaser the forgiveness of all sins committed afterward—no repentance was required. ("Certificates of Pardon" was a blemish on Christianity widely used by Muslims to make a mockery of the faith.)

Some of Luther's own congregation bought certificates of pardon and expected their pastor to offer them absolution. Luther refused. The Pope ordered that "all heretics who presumed to oppose his most holy indulgences" should be burned. *Ibid., 115.*

The reformer declared that only repentance toward God and faith in Jesus Christ could save. But the grace of Christ is a free gift and can not be purchased with money.

In a few days Luther's theses spread throughout all of Germany. In a few weeks they were heard throughout Christendom.

The wide spread of Luther's theses put him on a direct path for collision with the papists.

To enlighten the people "would be virtually to undermine the authority of Rome." *Ibid., 118.* Less treasury meant less luxury for the papal leaders. Looking for Christ alone would deprive Rome of its power and hegemony over the life of the people. The pontiff's throne was in great and immediate jeopardy.

Martin Luther was called a heretic.

Many who were enslaved by formalism clamored for his blood. "Many, however, who had received from Luther the precious light... suffered torture and death." *Ibid., 119.*

A summons was sent to Luther to go to Rome to address the charge of heresy. His friends begged him not to go to the city "already drunk with the blood of the martyrs of Jesus." *Ibid.* They requested his examination to be done in Germany.

The pontiff agreed.

His legate was told that Luther "had already been declared a heretic." *Ibid.* The judgment was pronounced before the hearing.

If Rome's representative could not gain possession of Luther, he was "empowered to proscribe him in every part of Germany; to banish, curse, and excommunicate all those who are attached to him." D'AUBIGNE, Chapter 2. *Ibid., 120.*

Such cruelty may not be unfamiliar to man. But when the "representative of God on earth" himself displays this spirit, something must be wrong. And this severity to be committed in the name of the Lord Jesus Christ, the lamb of God who forgave even those who put Him on the Cross, is beyond comprehension.

The reformer did not get a promise of safe-conduct. The legate planned to force Luther to retract his theses. Failing that, he would "cause him to be conveyed to Rome, to share the fate of Huss and Jerome." *Ibid., 121.*

Luther expressed his respect for the Church. He offered to submit his theses to the review of certain leading universities. But he could not retract them without "having proved him in error."

Finally he got permission to present his views in writing.

The prelate was confronted with Luther's strong reasoning and could not assail his doctrine. So in a rage he cried out,

> Retract! or I will send you to Rome, there to appear before the judges commissioned to take cognizance of your cause. I will excommunicate you and all your partisans, and all who shall at any time countenance you, and will cast them out of the church. *Ibid., 122.*

The reformer withdrew. This meant no retraction was expected from him.

The escape of Luther infuriated the legate.

He expressed his outrage in a letter to Frederick, the elector of Saxony, demanding that "Frederick send the reformer to Rome or banish him from Saxony." *Ibid., 123.*

Frederick was not fully familiar at the time with Luther's doctrines but was impressed by his clear words and candor. "Until the reformer should be proved in error, Frederick resolved to stand as his protector." *Ibid.*

The prince of Saxony ignored the legate's request to send Luther to Rome or expel him from his states.

Up to this point in time the reformer was still in support of the Roman Church. His writings spread to Switzerland, Holland, France, Spain, England, Belgium, and Italy itself.

This was too much for Rome to tolerate. Some of his opponents, including professors in Catholic universities, declared that "who should kill the rebellious monk would be without sin." *Ibid., 125.*

Such was the savagery of *man--n*ot ordinary men, but theological intellectuals.

The Bohemian reformer wrote to the universities, "Every institution in which men are not increasingly occupied with the word of God must become corrupt," <u>D'AUBIGNE</u>, Chapter 3. *Ibid., 126.*

Many people all over Germany were roused to rally around the words of Luther.

It did not take long for the Pope to declare that Luther's doctrine must be condemned. The reformer and his followers were granted 60 days to recant. If they did not, they "were all to be excommunicated." *Ibid.*

The impact on the Reformation movement was seriously felt. Rome's sentence of excommunication struck terror in the hearts of powerful monarchs across Europe. The Pope's power had no limits—geographically or spiritually. People knew that the mandate of Rome implied prison, torture, and the sword. Obedience was not unexpected.

"But Luther was fearless still." *Ibid., 127.*

In a crowd of students, professors, and citizens of all ranks, he burned the Pope's bull, the canon laws, and some writings supporting the papal power.

It must have taken a lot of internal struggle for Martin Luther to decide upon a final separation from the Roman Church.

The Pope's threat of excommunicating the reformer was now in effect.

> A new bull appeared, declaring the reformer's final separation from the Roman Church, denouncing him as accursed of heaven, and including in the same condemnation all who should receive his doctrines. *Ibid., 128.*

A long, gloomy chapter in the Church's history had been closed, and the Reformation was born to live and spread. Tyranny—even in the name of the Creator—had been condemned by Heaven.

To reiterate, the Dark Ages could be thought of as a blemish on Christianity, but the truth is that *man,* placed in a position of no accountability, is likely to abuse his power. The heart is deceitful, and

Satan uses every trick in his arsenal to play with the mind under the pretext of achieving a lofty goal.

Our Lord knew man's weakness and, as He promised His disciples, sent the Holy Spirit to live on the inside of those who believe in Him. Our refuge is near but he does not force His will upon us.

God bestowed freedom on man to choose for <u>himself</u> either to listen to Satan or to the Holy One.

<u>PROVERBS</u> 22:4 says, By humility *and* the fear of the LORD *are* riches, and honor, and life.

CHAPTER 2

IN ISLAM

Since creation God has bestowed power on man. How man handled that power was mainly shaped by his perception of the Creator.

Chapter 1 discussed the cloud that shrouded Christianity for the earlier centuries.

Nothing in the Bible condones the actions of the Roman Church under the Pope. The absolute power entrusted to man stands in clear contrast to the teachings of the message of peace, love, and forgiveness.

The opposite narrative describes Islam and its history.

The Qur'an as well as history point toward a message of war and coercion.

From the dawn of Islam all the way until recent times, conflict, fighting, and killing were the dominant themes interrupted by quiet periods only when the "Umma" (nation) of Islam was weak. No person could be singled out as responsible for the violence exhibited over most of the fourteen centuries of Islamic history. It is the *message* itself that has at its core hatred, war, conquering, and subjugation.

At the risk of upsetting the chronological sequence of events, note an article that appeared in August, 2016, in THE WALL STREET JOURNAL.

"A Sudanese man was killed in a clash with other migrants near the port of Calais," the French coastal town located on the English Channel. The man was killed after violence erupted between Sudanese and Afghanis. It was not an anomaly; the killing marked the "11th migrant fatality since January in the area."

The French police reported that 6,900 migrants from Sudan, Afghanistan, Syria, and Iraq "are living in makeshift camps in and around Calais.... Every night several hundred migrants attempt to stow away on trucks leading to the U. K. by boat or train, leading to violence with police and among migrants." *Ibid.*

Sudan, Afghanistan, Syria, and Iraq are countries with a Muslim majority. Migrants fleeing these countries choose to go to Europe to live among Christians. Why do they seek asylum in the land of infidels?

Saudi Arabia (19 million citizens in 2013) has tremendous resources and space to accommodate millions upon millions of fellow Muslims. But neither Saudi Arabia nor the migrants welcomes such a deal.

As a would-be host, Saudi Arabia, or any of the oil-rich Gulf States, is not willing to accept any Muslim migrants (obviously no Christians either).

The Saudis and other rich monarchs know quite well that allowing Muslim migrants in their country would bring nothing but trouble. The migrants themselves are hesitant to try to enter. Fleeing the civil war in Syria, many went to Lebanon (traditionally a Christian nation) or Jordan (a moderate Islamic country).

Here a question springs to mind.

Thousands upon thousands fled their war-torn Muslim nations mainly to Europe. Many of them even received welfare assistance from the host countries. Did such hospitality and generosity help? Did it attract job-seeking, tax-paying newcomers who intended to blend into the social fabric of their new-found homes?

"In March [2016], terrorist Khalid el-Bakraoui blew himself up inside Brussels' Maelbeek subway station, and 16 people died," <u>THE WALL STREET JOURNAL</u>, August 6-7, 2016, p. A12. Bakraoui has been imprisoned in Belgium for carjacking and armed robbery. He was released from prison early in 2014 and, according to Belgium's welfare system, got $28,000 in "various benefits."

Terror attacks in November 2015 in Paris killed 130 people. Two of the perpetrators were Salah Abdeslam and his brother Brahim Abdeslam. Salah was "collecting unemployment benefits until three weeks before the attack."

French authorities found in their possession an Islamic State manual titled "How to Survive in the West: A Mujahid Guide."

Potential jihadists are told "If you can claim extra benefits from a government, then do so."

If such actions seem unbelievable to us, it should not be surprising to those who are familiar with Islamic core beliefs.

Some Muslims believe that money, women, and even the life of infidels is free for the taking.

ISIL (or ISIS), Al-Quaeda, and the Muslim Brotherhood—disguised as a peaceful organization—took the mantra a step further. Not just infidels but also Shia Muslims, moderate Muslims, and anyone who is not jihadist *enough* is not worth living.

In November 2015 in the Inland Regional Center at San Bernardino, California, Rizwan Farook and his wife Tashfeen Malik killed 14 people and injured 24.

In June 2016 Omar Mateen, a 29-year-old security guard born in America, killed 49 people and wounded 53 others at Pulse, a gay nightclub in Orlando, Florida.

On July 14, 2016, Nice, France, witnessed the killing of 86 pedestrians celebrating Bastille Day and 434 were injured. A jihadist named Mohamed Lahouaiej-Bouhlel drove his truck through people walking on the Promenade des Anglais.

Over the span of nine months, from November 2015 until July 2016, 295 people were killed by Islamic terrorists in Europe and the United States and 511 were injured.

Within two weeks in the summer of 2017 terrorists attacked Manchester and then London. In Manchester 22 were killed, and seven were killed in London. Dozens more were injured.

On June 4, 2017, Theresa May, U. K. prime minister, called for allied democratic countries to unite in preventing terrorists from access to the Internet.

These were evil deeds committed by *men* who believe that Allah calls them to kill in his name. Their core beliefs are derived from the Qur'an and Hadith. The long history of Islam supports this line of hatred and killing of conquered nations unless they convert to Islam. The early stages of aggression and killing that accompanied the spread of Islam have continued in varying degrees from the seventh century until the present.

Sadly the world is seeing another wave of Islamic tide full of cruelty and barbaric actions from burning people alive in a cage (a Jordanian pilot) to the public beheading of 19 Egyptian Christians working in Libya.

Western leaders who see the danger of Islamic extremism are facing opposition from political opponents who sense an opportunity to gain some ground. Europe, in particular, seems to be in a state of paralysis and disarray as attacks continue and the number of victims mounts.

For a long time the West, and in particular America, decided to separate religion and state. In the mind of many, religion has been relegated to the personal: You may practice your own religion but it is to be kept private.

The problem here is that Islam views religion to be at the center of life—all public policy and personal beliefs are intertwined. A jihadist considers it legitimate to do everything at his disposal to defend Islam. If this means killing infidels, so be it. First they hijacked airplanes, then used explosive belts around their bodies, then turned to using trucks or vehicles as weapons of choice. Evil has no limits.

By killing non-Muslims, a jihadist is defending his "religion" against those who do not believe in Allah.

Westerners should realize that the loyalty of a Muslim is first and foremost to Islam. This loyalty supersedes loyalty to the host country s/he lives in, friends, and even close family members including parents, brothers, or sisters.

When the West opens its doors to followers of Islam, gratitude takes second or even third place.

Once brainwashed, a jihadist does not think of the goodness and generosity of the host country. Killing in the name of Allah overwhelms both the conscious and the subconscious blinding the mind and obscuring logic.

There may be no surprises here. This is just the way the thought process goes. The Qur'an makes it clear that when you die as a martyr "defending" the accepted religion of Allah, heaven is the reward where 70 (or 72) virgins will be waiting to entertain you.

Satan must be happy as he toys with the mind of *man* as he has always done since the creation.

Here is the question now facing Western leaders: Does a cost/benefit analysis favor bringing in more followers of Islam without extreme vetting?

Politics aside, the answer is emphatically no.

Recently the German prime minister decided to accept one million immigrants fleeing from Africa and Middle Eastern countries with the idea of having additional work force that the economy can absorb and benefit from.

Whether the one million undocumented immigrants have proved to be a positive economic asset is yet to be seen. But what is evident are the complaints of local females about several cases of rape and sexual assault by the newcomers.

As mentioned earlier, it is the message of Islam itself that is problematic. No single person can be blamed for the atrocities committed in the name of the faith over the centuries. What makes it even more tragic is that violence and hatred are not restricted to the Christian infidels.

THE ATLANTIC magazine, May 2016, pp. 78-90, reported on the suffering of a *Sunni* family by the *Sunni* ISIL terrorist group.

The Sunni Sabras family lived in a village in Anbar province, located in central Iraq.

When ISIL seized their village, they blew up houses and executed civilians as they fled.

"A few hundred families had managed to escape and were now scattered across Iraq." *Ibid.*

The Sabras family thought that they were lucky to land in Baghdad which was under complete control of anti-ISIL forces. At the time the capital of Iraq was predominantly Shia.

Within a short period of time the Sabras family realized that they were wrong. As ISIL spread its extremism, "their new Shia neighbors seemed to cast blame on *all* Sunnis, even those who had lost homes or loved ones to ISIL." *Ibid.*

Hatred can blind the mind.

Around Baghdad the Shia militia as well as the Iraqi army picked up Sunnis who were "never seen again." *Ibid*. For starters this meant they were tortured then executed.

The divide between the Shias and Sunnis in Iraq has been deepened because of the Islamic State in Iraq and other insurgent groups "through a campaign of violence targeting Shia civilians." *Ibid*. Although the Shia versus Sunni conflict extends throughout almost all of the history of Islam, the fight intensified after December 2011 when the Americans withdrew from Iraq.

In Islam old animosities never die; conflict continues forever.

Following the demise of Saddam Hussein's regime in 2003—a Sunni who brutalized the Shia majority—the Americans, through elections, put the Shia majority in power. Instead of allowing Sunnis to share in governing Iraq, the Shias embarked on a campaign to persecute the Sunnis. It was pay-back time. And the Sunnis responded with bloody attacks against the Shias and their shrines.

In response to the Sunni mayhem, the Iraqi State carried out raids and arrests that "swept up innocent Sunnis.... Thousands were imprisoned or disappeared on dubious grounds." *Ibid*. The police beat women and tortured them with electric shocks. This brutality came not from a terrorist group but from men in uniform. In April 2013 security forces killed at least 50 and injured more than 100 protesters in the town of Hawija.

In many towns Sunni tribes engaged in open warfare with the Iraqi State.

> For a while, a tenuous alliance of Sunni tribes, ISIL, and other revolutionary groups held together. But ISIL began murdering its *allies* in order to dominate the movement, and... the Iraqi State increased its repression.... The Sunni alliance crumbled, forcing some sheikhs to flee and others to join ISIL for protection.... [In] this fractured environment... ISIL began swallowing up large parts of western Iraq. *Ibid*.

In 2014 ISIL got control of Fallujah, and a few months later the group invaded Mosul, the second-largest city in Iraq after Baghdad. (The terrorist group remained in Mosul till the summer of 2017 when the national army of Iraq advised by Americans expelled them from their stronghold. Mosul has been effectively demolished.)

The fighting forced some Sunni families to be caught between ISIL on one side and the U.S. and allied forces (the Iraqi army and Shia militia) on the other.

For Iraqi civilians "the anti-ISIL forces are just as violent and oppressive as the entity they are fighting." *Ibid.* Cruelty is second nature for most Iraqi people—Sunnis as well as Shias.

Falah Sabras joined the police force. His police station was just outside Zweiya.

In October 2014 ISIL forces besieged the police station, and gave the policemen 24 hours to flee but they had to leave the women, children, and the elderly behind.

They did and ISIL captured Zweiya without a shot fired.

For two days those left behind were treated well. One evening a man on a loudspeaker riding in an ISIL Humvee announced that "anyone with a relative who had worked with the Americans or the Iraqi government... would have 24 hours to evacuate." *Ibid.*

But, those leaving had to leave their cars and take only what they could carry.

Many families from Zweiya ended up in refugee camps. Because Falah was a policeman he was able to resettle in Haditha (a town 50 miles away) in the house of a fellow tribesman. "With the influx of refugees... and the battles raging nearby," food prices shot skyward. *Ibid.* A broker friend found a house in Baghdad for Falah's family.

In April 2015 ISIL instructed the Sabras to leave Baghdad.

The men who came to the Sabras' door tied Falah's hands, closed his eyes with a blindfold, and filled his mouth with cloth. The intruders forced adult men into a room; women and children were herded downstairs. Then the men were led outside and shot.

Somehow Falah survived. He fled to Kurdistan to live with his cousin and best friend, Abu Ammar.

Doctors in Kurdistan found that a bullet had passed through his neck causing damage to his cranial nerves. They believed he may lose his speech permanently. He has lost vision in his left eye and hearing in his left ear.

Although no accurate numbers "exist as to how many Sunnis have been killed by anti-ISIL forces... human rights workers... allege that... anti-ISIL forces may have killed as many Sunnis as ISIL has." *Ibid.*

A worker at a Non Governmental Organization in Baghdad told <u>THE ATLANTIC</u> reporter,

> After the fall of Mosul to ISIL in 2014, she learned that hundreds of Sunnis had been rounded up and disappeared by Iraqi forces outside Baghdad. Following the fall of Ramadi one year later, Shiite militias similarly took revenge on Sunni refugees in the capital [Baghdad]....
> According to a 2015 UN human rights report, anti-ISIL forces seemed to be acting with 'total impunity,' leaving a trail of death and destruction in their wake.

Actually, the trail of death and destruction has been shared more or less equally by the two major sects of the same religion: Islam. It may not be easy to figure out which sect has outnumbrered the other in killing.

Some Shia militias matched ISIL in their brutality. A video showed a militia commander who "strung up a burnt man" and sliced him like kabab. Another video featured fighters who "beheaded and disemboweled two captives." *Ibid.*

At the morgue dozens of maimed and discolored bodies showed up each week.

Oh, for the brutality of *man.*

The Islamic State's strategy is to frighten and terrorize the Shia communities. Shia militias feel it is payback time for the savagery of Saddam's regime when the Sunni government kept tight control over the Shias who constitute the majority of the Iraqi population.

The Kurds, too, did not escape Saddam's rule of terror. With American support, the Kurds now enjoy a semi-autonomous state in northern Iraq.

Robert D. Kaplan, senior fellow at the Center for a New American Security, describes how Islam split the Mediterranean world in two. He writes, "For centuries in early and middle antiquity, Europe meant the world surrounding the Mediterranean, or Mare Nostrum (Our Sea), as the Romans famously called it." THE ATLANTIC, May 2016, pp. 22-23.

At the time Europe included North Africa.

Saint Augustine lived in what is now Algeria—a center of Christianity, just as Greece or Italy. Alexandria, Egypt, was considered the center of Christianity in the earlier centuries A.D. before Saint Augustine. The Library of Alexandria was the equivalent of the present-day Library of Congress. Saint Mark came to Alexandria around 69 A.D. and preached Christianity. Egypt became a Christian nation until the Arabs conquered it in the seventh century.

In the seventh and eighth centuries the armies of Islam conquered all of North Africa: Egypt, Libya, Tunisia, Algeria, and Morocco. This, in effect, severed "the Mediterranean region into two civilizational halves," with the Sea separating—rather than unifying—them. *Ibid.*

Kaplan then describes how the modern European state system developed slowly and "gave way to early modern empires and, over time, to nationalism and democracy." *Ibid.*

So, "the West" emerged in Europe essentially after Islam had split the Mediterranean world. One might add that over time the splitting freed Europe from the shackles of Islam that held North African nations dysfunctional both socially and economically to this day. Even Egypt, a country with a splendid civilization that extended back five thousand years B.C., fell under the hegemony of the invading Arabs.

Islam is not just a "religion." It is a culture of its own; it encompasses all aspects of the life of its adherents.

At its inception in the seventh century, the Prophet Mohammed was the military leader, head of state, and inspirational source for the "nation" or "Umma" of Islam. The spread of Islam did not have "choice" as an option for those overtaken by the armies of Islam during the seventh and eighth centuries. The conquered *had* to "choose" between converting to Islam, paying a special exorbitant tax "Gizya", or being beheaded.

It has rightfully been said that Islam and democracy did not, could not, and would not mix.

Kaplan cites the book by Denys Hay, a British historian, that was published in 1957 and titled <u>EUROPE: THE EMERGENCE OF AN IDEA.</u> "European unity began with the concept... of a Christendom in 'inevitable opposition' to Islam."

The scholar Edward Said in his book <u>ORIENTALISM</u>, published in 1978, says that "Islam had defined Europe culturally, by showing Europe what it is against."

During the colonial era, modern Europe conquered the Middle East. Napoleon, towards the end of the eighteenth century, "dispatched scholars... to study Islamic civilization, classifying it as something beautiful, fascinating, and—most crucial—inferior."

With the Industrial Revolution (1760-1840), Europe progressed culturally, scientifically, economically, and socially; its preeminence was fortified.

In North Africa and the Levant, rulers of the Muslim-majority countries adopted dictatorship as the means to control their people. Kept as prisoners inside secure boarders, "the Arab populations had bartered away their political freedom for economic protection." THE WALL STREET JOURNAL, July 8, 2011, p. A15.

And for many, economic protection proved elusive.

Middle Eastern countries with limited or no natural resources, such as Egypt, Jordan, and Syria are suffering economically.

Oil-rich nations keep their citizens happy by distributing oil money. Over the past six or seven decades of overflowing oil, little or no industrial projects emerged. What would happen to the Gulf States after oil is drained or demand plummets is anyone's guess.

Actually, a preview is now in motion. After oil prices hit $140 a barrel a few years ago, increased oil production by American companies using "fracking" led to a price hovering between 40 and 50 dollars a barrel.

Recently the Saudi government released $1 billion to help laid-off workers, THE WALL STREET JOURNAL, October 3, 2016, p. A12. The government paid this money to two of its biggest construction firms. "Unpaid or out-of-work laborers have staged sporadic protests, including setting fire to company buses in Mecca." The steep slump in oil prices is causing a cash crunch resulting from a "dramatic scaling back of government spending."

Robert Kaplan then addresses the present-day consequences of unsuccessful policies in North Africa, the Middle East, and other Muslim-majority countries,

> Today, hundreds of thousands of Muslims who have
> no desire to be Christian are filtering into economically
> stagnant European states, threatening to undermine the
> fragile social peace. Though Europe's elites have for decades
> used idealistic rhetoric to deny the forces of religion
> and ethnicity, those were the very forces that provided
> European States with their own internal cohesion. THE
> ATLANTIC, May 2016, pp. 22-23.

Whereas European, and to a lesser extent, American elites try to deny forces of religion when dealing with Islam and Muslims, the fact remains that the latter see life only through the lens of religion. As noted earlier, the loyalty of a Muslim is first and foremost to his/her religion.

How Europe deals with the influx of so many Muslims "who have no desire to be Christian," and whose culture stands in direct contrast to the West's Christian core values of freedom, human rights, and rule of law is an ongoing challenge.

From among all who write about the customs and history of Islamic society, Bernard Lewis stands out.

He is "justly regarded as the world's premier living authority on the history of the Middle East and the Arab world." National Review, commenting on the book THE CRISIS OF ISLAM, Bernard Lewis, Random House, New York, 2003.

Bernard Lewis writes, "For bin Ladin and those who follow him, this is a religious war, a war for Islam against infidels, and therefore, inevitably, against the United States, the greatest power in the world of infidels.", *Ibid.,* xv.

For some in America and the West to see this war differently is both misguided as well as dangerous.

The author of this book was born and lived for 40 years in the Middle East, principally in Egypt. As a Christian living in a Muslim-majority country, he has a first-hand awareness of how Islam perceives the world and the responsibility laid on every Muslim to spread the "correct" religion allover the world by *all* possible means.

The end overrides the means. Killing, bombing, lying, and deceiving are all permissible in pursuit of the ultimate goal of having Islam as the dominant and only religion. Once Islam takes over, *all* the world's problems would be solved.

But reality defies this unsubstantiated assumption.

If Muslim-majority countries the world over are underdeveloped and lagging economically and intellectually, how could Islam solve the world's problems when it is failing in its own jurisdiction?

It seems *man* has the uncanny ability to deceive himself and possibly others.

In an October 2001 videotape of the late bin Ladin, he mentions the "humiliation and disgrace" that Islam has suffered for "more than eighty years." THE CRISIS OF ISLAM, p. xv. Implied in the video is an intent on revenge.

The end of WWI put an end to the Ottoman Sultanate, the "last of the great Muslim empires." *Ibid, xvi.* The former Ottoman territories, commonly referred to as the Fertile Crescent, were divided into three entities.

Iraq and Palestine were put under British mandate; Syria was given to the French. Sometime later the French subdivided Syria in half: one part was called Lebanon and the rest retained the name Syria. The British did the same in Palestine. The Jordan river marked the division of Palestine in half: east of the Jordan river was called Jordan, and the western segment retained the name Palestine.

At the time the Arabian peninsula, mainly barren and inaccessible deserts, was "thought not worth the trouble of taking over." *Ibid.*

Obviously this turned out to be a big mistake. The discovery of vast oil resources by the end of WWII converted the desert into high rises and modern malls. Saudi Arabia and the other Gulf States accumulated great wealth, and with it came a favorable political status on the world stage.

The defeat of the Ottomans in WWI was counterbalanced by the rising power of the Gulf States after WWII. Islam got a strong push forward, and a wave of Islamic tide dominated the latter part of the twentieth century and continues today.

The Turks, under the Ottoman general known as Kemal Ataturk, got their freedom not in the name of Islam but by adopting Western culture. Ataturk preferred to call his policies "modern ways." In November 1922 he abolished the sultanate. In March 1924 the Turks abolished the caliphate, too.

The defeat and disintegration of the Ottoman empire marked the end of a long era that extended back to the death of the Prophet Mohammed in 632 A.D.

After his death a successor was appointed to take his place, "not as spiritual but as religious and political head of the Muslim state and community." *Ibid., xvii.*

Over nearly thirteen centuries the caliphate remained a "potent symbol of Muslim unity, even identity; its disappearance, under the double assault of foreign imperialists and domestic modernists, was felt throughout the Muslim world." *Ibid.*

As the caliphate ended in 1924, the fight for defending and preserving Islam has been delegated to individuals to carry the banner of the only "right" religion. Gone were the times when a nation symbolized the "Umma" of Islam.

In Egypt, Hassan El Banna answered the call of Allah.

In 1928 he established what has been known as the Muslim Brotherhood organization. Started as a social group providing medical and financial assistance only to fellow Muslims, it morphed into a political, secretive organization.

Over time the Brotherhood gained strength. In the late 1940s it managed to assassinate the Egyptian prime minister.

The book <u>TWO DIFFERENT RELIGIONS. HOW ISLAM PERCEIVES CHRISTIANITY AND WHAT IS THE TRUTH</u>, Safwat Bishara. Authorhouse, Bloomington, Indiana, 2013, states

> This set in motion an awareness by the authorities of the ambitions and dangers of the secretive organization. In 1954, they tried and failed to assassinate the leader of the 1952 revolution—the late President Nasser—as he was delivering a speech in Al Manshia square, Alexandria. The powerful president aimed to completely eradicate the religion-turned-terrorist group. Many of its members were jailed, while others fled Egypt to neighboring Muslim countries, notably Saudi Arabia.

As it turned out later, the Muslim Brotherhood organization had never died out. Its hierarchial, secretive structure allowed it to go underground in anticipation of the right moment. (Even Saudi Arabia, who hosted the fleeing members, banned it as a terrorist organization in 2014.)

Gamal Abd El Nasser strongly believed in Pan-Arabism. He himself was not a fanatic, but his policy of uniting Arab nations against the West meant, for many, jihad in the name of Islam—a notion and belief that is as old as Islam itself.

In 1962 Mummar El Gaddafi, a Libyan army colonel, overthrew the government of King Idris El Senousi and took control of Libya, the country that borders Egypt to the west. Gaddafi looked up to Nasser for inspiration; both shared youth, military background, ambition, and Pan-Arabism.

The region started to cohere around the rhetoric of Pan-Arabism, favored by a common language and, more crucially, by a common belief in Islam.

But did it really? Can *man* overcome feelings of selfishness and self-interest even for the sake of his country?

A short-lived union between Egypt and Syria ended on a sour note for both countries.

Other Arab leaders could not conceive of going into a union with the more populous and intellectually superior Egypt led by a charismatic, strong man like Nasser.

In the early 1960s Egypt got into a quagmire by getting involved in the war in Yemen that cost Egypt a lot of blood and money with nothing gained.

Nasser passed away in 1970. After him Anwar El Sadat, one of the twelve free army officers who overthrew the Egyptian government in 1952, became Egypt's president.

After the death of Nasser, Gaddafi, who was considered a son by Nasser, aspired to be the president of both Libya (six million people) and Egypt (about 50 million at the time). He even threatened to use the Libyan armed forces to compel Egypt into accepting his presidency.

The dream did not last long however.

Sadat, seeing that Gaddafi was serious in his pursuit, made him an offer.

Gaddafi was invited to meet and discuss with a group of about 20 or so who represented the Egyptian intelligentsia. Gaddafi declined, and the idea was forever forgotten.

During the 1960s and 1970s Pan Arabism continued—as a slogan.

Not far from the Middle East, the Iranians jumped on the wagon of jihad. In 1979 El Khomenei, the Shia Mulla in exile in France for years, came back to Tehran where he was received with great enthusiasm as the spiritual leader of the Iranian revolution.

The abolition of the caliphate in 1924 by the Turks may not have been the end of the "Umma" of Islam. Organizations like the Muslim Brotherhood in Egypt, as well as nations such as Libya and Iran, have revived the hope of some that Muslim-majority nations would unite under a caliph just as it was at the dawn of Islam.

Some recent successive events have actually helped create a caliphate in Iraq—a flimsy one indeed, but a dream coming true for jihadists.

Abu-Bakr El Baghdadi crowned himself caliph. His organization, ISIL or ISIS, has proved itself to be a most vicious, cruel, and barbarian, terrorist group. Beheading and burning alive in a cage are just a sample of its message of terror. Coercion and intimidation are the hallmarks of the caliphate of the twenty-first century just as it was in the seventh and eighth centuries.

Evil persists ever since Adam and Eve.

The problem here is not as much in *man* as it is in the message of Islam itself.

This brutality stands in stark contrast to the message of Christianity—a message that has peace, love, and forgiveness at its core. However some Christian men sought power and overstepped their boundaries in an era that came to be marked as the Dark Ages. But then God sent men like John Wycliffe in England, John Huss in Bohemia, and Martin Luther in Germany. These men stood firm in their beliefs and felt compelled to defend the Word of God even at the expense of their lives. The Reformation, then the Enlightenment, released human capacity, and Europe flourished economically, socially, militarily, and intellectually.

Islam affects its followers in a peculiar way. Bernard Lewis writes

The Muslim peoples, like everyone else in the world, are shaped by their history, but unlike some others, they are keenly aware of it. Their awareness dates however from the advent of Islam, with perhaps some minimal reference to pre-Islamic times,.... Islamic history, for Muslims, has an important religious and also legal significance, since it reflects the working out of God's [Allah] purpose for His community. THE CRISIS OF ISLAM, p. xix.

Islamic history, for Muslims, is not the past but an inspiration for the present and a source of dreams for the future. This may explain the emergence of ISIL under a caliph, a century after the Turks abolished the caliphate. The dream continues and never dies.

As Lewis keenly points out, even in "countries of ancient civilization like those of the Middle East, the knowledge of pagan history—of their own ancestors, whose monuments and inscriptions lay around them—was minimal." *Ibid.* Syria, Iraq, and Egypt are good examples.

The author of this work was born in Egypt and lived there most of his first forty years. At school students learn a great deal about Islamic history and all the details about how the armies of Allah conquered nations east, north, and west of the Arabian peninsula.

The Muslim armies overthrew the Persian empire and "incorporated all its territories in the domains of the caliphate, opening the way to the invasion of Central Asia and of India." *Ibid., 34.*

Syria and Iraq were taken as well as all of North Africa—Egypt, Libya, Tunisia, Algeria, and Morocco—before crossing the Mediterranean Sea to Spain. All were taken over a period of about a century from the mid-seventh to the mid-eighth century.

On the other hand, Egyptian students have but a scant glimpse into the great civilization of Ancient Egypt. It is as if the history of Egypt starts with the advent of Islam when their armies conquered Egypt in 642 A.D. and not several millennia before.

"From 3100 B.C. to 1100 B.C., the ancient Egyptian civilization introduced to humanity writing, medical science, architecture, a mature art, gigantic monuments, comfortable furnishings, and a distinctive attitude toward death which they viewed as an extension of life." Safwat Bishara and Dawlat Bishara. ABOUT LEARNING AND EDUCATION. A PARENT AND EDUCATOR'S VIEW SUPPORTED BY OVERSEAS EXPERIENCE, Authorhouse, Bloomington, Indiana, 2015, pp. 163-164.

John A. Wilson, professor of Egyptology at the University of Chicago, writes

> The Hebrews, the Greeks, and the Romans were much impressed by ancient Egypt, and some of them paid respectful credit to that culture for learning and skill. If we are closer in understanding to the Hebrews, the Greeks, and the Romans, we must remember that the Egyptians established the essentials of their culture two thousand years before these later peoples. *Ibid., 160.*

Almost four millennia of a remarkable history prior to Islam are mostly ignored as irrelevant.

Tourists from allover the world travel to see the magnificent, gigantic, and beautiful statutes and monuments in Egypt.

And it is not just the history of ancient Egypt that is being neglected. A six-century period of Egypt's past is completely omitted from history books.

Around 67 A.D., Saint Mark arrived in Alexandria, Egypt. He started preaching Christianity, and over time Egypt became a Christian nation.

Sad to say, but the present author—a Christian—only recently became aware of this early dominance of Christianity in Egypt, and it was not at school.

For a short period of time the Muslim Brotherhood came to power in Egypt, and it was only after a controversial election. From June 2012 until July 3rd, 2013, Mohammed Morsi, the presidential candidate of the party of Freedom and Justice—the political arm of the Brothers—became Egypt's president.

Feeling empowered, the fanatics started talking about destroying monuments, such as the Pyramids, and the Sphinx, under the pretense that these are idols not to be worshiped. Or, at a minimum, the statutes should be covered. (Note that this is the same mentality that destroyed ancient, historical monuments in Syria and Iraq by ISIL.)

Luckily for all humanity and for Egypt, the Egyptian military stood firm, responding to the call of 30 million citizens who protested against Islamic extremists who exposed their perverted view of the world.

Since its inception in 1928, the Muslim Brotherhood organization claimed to be a peaceful entity. For decades the majority of Muslims felt sympathy for them as they claimed to be victims. The norm is that a Muslim sympathizes with other Muslims. But after holding the presidency in 2012, it became apparent to almost all Muslims that the organization was only after its own power at the exclusion of everyone else, even the other Muslim groups such as the Salafis. Their backward mentality sought to ban movies (except with male actors only), singing, and ballet dancing (because they claim ballet dancers perform naked).

The Egyptians rejected the seventh-century culture of Arabia.

Syria was not as fortunate as Egypt. Egyptians are more or less homogeneous. With very few exceptions all Muslims are Sunnis and all Christians are Coptic Orthodox, and this helped in maintaining unity of the country.

Syria, like other Arab countries, has Sunnis and Shias with varying proportions and some Christians as a minority.

In 2011 the year ascribed to the Arab Spring (which proved elusive), insurgents infiltrated Syria.

President Bashar El Assad, an Alawi—a sect of Shia Islam—became the target of Sunni Muslims. Money, weapons, and possibly fighters poured in from the oil-rich Gulf States.

Led by Saudi Arabia, the United Arab Emirates (U.A.E.), and Qatar, the Sunni Muslims are fighting a proxy war against the Shias in Syria. Iran, Iraq, and Hezbulla in Lebanon are supporting El Assad, the Shia president of Syria. And in the meantime, the country has been decimated.

The hatred and animosity between the two main sects of Islam has continued for centuries since the early days of Islam. Peace, love, and forgiveness have no much place in the vocabulary of a faith that claims to be "peaceful."

In Toronto an exhibition called "Syria A Living History" featured 48 objects from seven international museums. The Syrian-born co-curator, Nasser Rabbat, is professor of Islamic Art and Architecture at MIT. He said to Melik Kaylan of THE WALL STREET JOURNAL, "for most people Syria evokes images of chaos and destruction so we wanted to show a deeper perspective of Syria's contributions to civilization throughout history," October 18, 2016, p. D5.

In the exhibit is the 2012 painting "Deluge: The Gods Abandon Palmyra" that portrays "the varied species... saved from the biblical flood." *Ibid.*

Filiz C. Phillip, the co-curator of the museum said, "we wanted to show up front that creativity endures in the present. It is a dramatic start for any viewer who realizes that the powerful painting anticipated the despoiling of Palmyra by ISIL." *Ibid.*

Two different countries, Egypt and Syria, suffered from the same mentality that despises any culture that is not Islamic. The artifacts of any civilization that preceded Islam must be destroyed.

By the same token, any religion other than Islam has to be abolished. This is the duty of every Muslim to defend Islam against the imagined hostility of the infidels. ISIL of the twenty-first century carries almost the same message as that of the seventh and eighth centuries.

"In the early centuries of the Muslim era, the Islamic community was one state under one ruler. Even after that community split into many states, the ideal of a single Islamic polity persisted," writes Bernard Lewis. *Ibid., xxi.*

Indeed, the dream of "a single Islamic polity" is still alive and well even today.

After the "Arab Spring" started in 2011, the Islamist prime minister of Turkey, Recep Tayyip Erdogan, jumped to grab the opportunity of reviving the Ottoman empire. Iraq and Syria were in turmoil and in Egypt the Muslim Brotherhood was in control. The prevailing mood in the region appeared to support the resurgence of a single Islamic state, and Erdogan thought he should be the ruler of that empire.

But times have changed, and traditionally Islamic leaders do not have great trust in each other to voluntarily hand over their authority to another Muslim. Suspicion and thoughts of betrayal are not uncommon in the history of Islam.

And events on the ground proved that even today old attitudes still prevail.

On July 3rd, 2013, the Egyptian military kicked the Islamic regime out of office and arrested Mohammed Morsi and a number of his Brotherhood activists/thugs. The Islamic ex-president had been put to trial, found guilty, and imprisoned. He should have been grateful to have escaped the fate of other dictators, such as Saddam Hussein of Iraq and Moammar Gaddafi of Libya. The first was executed and the second bludgeoned, both by their oppressed peoples.

Erdogan tried repeatedly to interfere in neighboring Syria, but the Russians stood firm in supporting El Assad, the Syrian president.

Iraq was, and still is, in chaos. The Shia government, with major help from the U. S., has finally succeeded in dislodging the Sunni ISIL from Mosul and other parts of northern Iraq.

Erdogan's personal ambitions and hopes were dashed forever. In fact in June 2014, he had internal problems and protests that were followed by an alleged coup which led to the arrest of many army generals.

In 2014 Abu Bakr El Baghdadi stepped in to establish the never-forgotten goal of "a single Islamic polity." The United States, as well as Russia, seem determined to fight and demolish the terrorist organization that has lost most of its territories both in Iraq and Syria during 2017.

But the fact remains, for Muslims, the ideal is to have "one state under one ruler," just as it was in the early centuries of the Muslim era.

Over the centuries prior to the modern period, Islamic officials and historians "referred to their opponents not in... national terms but simply as infidels.... Similarly, they never referred to their own side as Arab, or Persian, or Turkish; they identified themselves as Muslims." Bernard Lewis, *Ibid., xxii.*

How significant for the West to be always aware of this train of thought: *All* non-Muslims fall in one class of infidels, and *all* Muslims are one regardless of their citizenship.

That feature of the Islamic culture illustrates the collective thinking that binds Muslims allover the world. It is socially accepted, even expected, that a Muslim must support his Muslim "brother" whether s/he is right or wrong. It does not matter what truth, honesty, or justice calls for.

Again, it is the message itself, rather than *man*, that is twisted.

To expect a Muslim family member, friend, or neighbor to inform local authorities about an illegal, destructive, or terrorist activity by a fellow Muslim living in the West is *not* going to happen. It simply runs against deep, strongly-held beliefs that go back for centuries.

51

For eight years, 1980 to 1988, war erupted between Iraq under Saddam, a Sunni, and Iran under the rule of the Shia mullahs. More than one million people were killed; some were in their teens.

Bernard Lewis writes, "both sides waged massive propaganda campaigns that frequently evoked events and personalities dating back as far as the seventh century." *Ibid., xxiii.*

For some, war may end but hatred and hostility persist for centuries, possibly forever.

Shias and Sunnis may, however, unite but only in their disdain for the infidels.

The violence that characterizes the relationship either between Shias and Sunnis or between Muslims and Christians and Jews could be viewed as a consequence of Islamic teachings that are devoid of love, peace, and forgiveness, which are considered nothing but signs of weakness. Young Muslim students are taught in school that the faith was spread by the power of the sword.

Some may argue that Christians have also fought long wars among themselves. That is true, but Christianity itself is a peaceful religion that was spread by humble followers of our Lord who were martyred for preaching the Word. Only John, the beloved, died in exile.

The long wars in Europe are in part a blemish on *men* with untamed ambitions and power-hungry personalities who happened to be "Christians."

Nevertheless, the last century has seen Europe embroiled in two world wars. A few years after the end of WWII, France and Germany, two fierce foes, took the first steps toward what would be the European Union.

Now 28 nations (27 after Brexit, following a June 2016 referendum) belong to the European Union. Cooperation replaced hostility and war. Agreement replaced conflict.

In another part of the world, the second half of the twentieth century ushered a period in the Middle East where "imperialism" caused the Arab states to collide with the West. It is imperialism that drew some countries together under the banner of Pan-Arabism.

Interestingly, when the armies of Allah conquered nations east, north, and west of the Arabian peninsula, they never referred to the Islamic empire as the product of imperialism. They actually believed that they were rendering a favor to the conquered people by forcing them to convert to the only "true" faith.

"In the Muslim perception, conversion to Islam is a benefit to the convert and a merit in those who convert him. In Islamic law, conversion *from* Islam is apostasy—a capital offense," writes Lewis,. *Ibid., 55.*

"While it was perfectly legitimate for Muslims to conquer and rule Europe," it was a crime and sin for "Europeans to conquer and rule" Islamic nations. *Ibid.*

How deceitful is the heart of *man,* and how twisted can his logic be.

Dr. Walid Phares, professor of Middle East Studies, Ethnic and Religious Conflict at Florida Atlantic University, in his book FUTURE JIHAD, TERRORIST STRATEGIES AGAINST THE WEST, Palgrave Macmillan, N. Y., 2005, says,

> The "system" at war with America is in fact centuries old and can not be defined solely in terms of countries, regimes, or leaders.... The jihadists' vision of defeat has not yet been understood by the West. Jihadists do not see the death of Osama [Bin Laden] or loss of Fallujah as a defeat.... In jihadists' view, Allah determines both victory and defeat.

Phares emphasizes the importance of understanding the historical roots of jihadism for the West to deal effectively with the threat.

Although the ideology was born a few decades ago, it was "inspired by doctrines from the Middle Ages." *Ibid.*

In its history America has never been engaged in a conflict with such deep roots. Jihadists' strategies are not based on classical state warfare. "The resources of regimes have been merged with the capabilities of networks." *Ibid.* Oil-rich monarchs and leaders are pouring out money to extremists who find it their "duty" to defend their faith against non-Muslims and even those who are not Islamic enough.

Fifteen of the 19 terrorists involved in the 9/11 attacks were from Saudi Arabia. Whether the Saudi regime provided help, information, or money has not been established. But the sheer number of Saudis responsible for the carnage poses serious doubts.

This may not be surprising when one considers what youngsters study in Saudi schools. The message, as well as the history, of Islam is replete with killings, murders, betrayals, and war. Of the first five rulers of the "Umma," three were murdered by Muslims.

And jihadists' destruction is not limited to the U.S. and Europe.

Iran is the chief supporter of terrorism allover the Middle East region. Hamas in the Gaza strip is a branch of the Muslim Brotherhood. Since the ouster in July 2013 of the Muslim Brotherhood president, Mohammed Morsi, from office by the Egyptian military, Egypt has been fighting a fierce battle against jihadists/terrorists in the Sinai peninsula.

The Egyptian government is standing firm in defending its citizens against insurgent terrorists from Hamas and the local Muslim Brotherhood terrorists who went underground after they lost office.

After the Gaddafi regime collapsed, Libya became a hotbed of terrorists. Chaos and turmoil turned this oil-rich country of six million into a dysfunctional nation.

In Mali, Al Quaeda allied with other Islamist extremists and took over more than half of this western African nation.

Nigeria, the most populous Islamic nation in Africa, has seen Boko Haram (translation: western teaching is sinful) terrorizes Christians in the northeastern part of the country. A few years ago more than 200 Christian girls were kidnapped to serve as sex slaves for the thugs.

Afghanistan and Pakistan have been engulfed in terrorist attacks both across their common border and within each country.

Pakistan hosted Bin Laden in a house not far from a major military installation, but Pakistanis denied any knowledge of his hiding place until he was killed.

Lying is religiously acceptable if it means protecting a fellow Muslim.

Russia fought Muslim separatists in Chechnya for years. The Chechens launched a number of terrorist attacks inside Russia killing scores of people.

"In Soviet times, Islam in Tatarstan was largely a means of ethnic identification.... Yet in recent years Salafism, which has gained followers throughout the Muslim world, has made inroads in Tatarstan." THE ECONOMIST, September 1, 2012, p.55. And the trouble began.

China, too, started to suffer from ethnic disturbances in provinces where Muslims used to live peacefully with others. The virus of jihadism is proving to be contagious.

From Asia, to Africa, to Europe, and to the U.S. the "war" continues. This is not a traditional war, but a new type of conflict with deep roots that extend back for centuries.

Unlike in Western culture, history lives forever in the Islamic mind.

In the 1950s, 1960s, and 1970s when the Middle East region witnessed direct or indirect military conflicts with the West, the mainstream media revived the history of the Crusaders, almost thousand years ago.

Living in the past with all of its conflicts and disagreements cripples a person as well as a nation.

The Creator knew man's weakness. Harboring a grudge is part of human nature. That is probably why our Lord Jesus Christ emphasized forgiveness. When Peter asked the Lord how many times he should forgive someone, seven times? The Lord answered, "Seventy times seven." The point is that there is no limit to forgiveness. But, this is Christianity.

The Bible says forgiveness pleases God. In the Lord's prayer the Christian asks God to forgive his/her trespasses just as s/he forgives those who trespass against him/her. Because forgiveness does not come naturally to *man*, the Lord's prayer is a daily reminder.

Forgiveness does not only please God, which is in itself the ultimate goal of man, but it is also good for the offended. To dwell on an offense only hurts the victim, straining his/her relationships with those around him, possibly causing physical ailments.

The epic of forgiveness has forever been exhibited on the Cross.

The Lord prayed to the Father to *forgive* those who were crucifying Him. Insults and torture causing excruciating pain preceded the piercing of His wrists and feet. Our Savior asked for forgiveness for those who knew not what they were doing.

Broadly speaking, the West adopted Christianity. Freedom, democracy, human rights, and the rule of law led to progress and prosperity.

Others believed in Islam. One-man or one-party rule bred dictatorships where freedom, human rights, and rule of law were inherently curtailed. Intimidation prevailed. Innovation disappeared. Societies refuse progress and tend to get stuck in the past.

PART II

PART II: POWER OF MONEY

"The love of money is the root of all evil," Paul wrote in <u>1 Timothy</u> 6:10.

The key word here is "love." Money is not a curse but a blessing if it is used according to the Word of God's principles.

J. C. Penney started his business from scratch. He kept for himself 90 percent of his revenue and donated 10 percent to the church. God blessed him. The 10 percent increased to 20 percent. God blessed him again, and J. C. Penney paid 30 percent to the work of God.

Without hesitation, he responded wisely to God's blessings and kept a smaller proportion of the revenue while increasing his contribution to the church.

Over time, Penney kept 10 percent and rendered 90 percent to God, the One who owns it all.

When Paul writes "the love of money is the root of all evil," he is cautioning *man* not to be lured into loving money more than loving the Creator who controls it all.

Man can not serve both God and money. He has to choose. <u>Matthew</u> 6:24 says, "No man can serve two masters: for either he will hate the one, and love the other; or else he will hold to the one, and despise the other. Ye cannot serve God and mammon."

To put it differently, one of God's blessings upon man may come in the form of money. The problem arises when man starts to "worship" money instead of the Provider.

CHAPTER 3

ON INDIVIDUALS

If you own a car, the manufacturer's manual is the guide to follow in order to keep the car in good condition.

If you are a researcher who works with scientific instruments and equipment, the manufacturer's instructions are essential tools if, and when, a malfunctioning apparatus quits working.

Because God created *man*, the Bible is the "manufacturer's manual."

Obviously, *man* is free to choose. He may or may not follow God's "instructions." And choices have consequences. The Holy Spirit, who resides within those who believe in Him, is man's helper to guide if he is willing to listen. There is no intimidation. The Creator does not need *man*, but *man* experiences the joy of fulfillment by following God's word.

An article in <u>THE ECONOMIST</u>, October 5, 2013, p. 86, quotes the Bible as Paul writes to Timothy, "The love of money is the root of all evil." It goes on to say that "all" may be "putting it a bit strongly, but dozens of psychological studies have indeed shown that people primed to think about money before an experiment are more likely to lie, cheat, and steal during the course of that experiment."

Like other researchers, psychologists carry out their experiments under controlled conditions. The setting limits the "choices" available to subjects as opposed to real-life situations. And yet studies "have indeed shown that people primed to think about money... are more likely to lie, cheat, and steal." *Ibid.* It seems logical then to conclude that more evil should occur given life's complexities and difficulties. In other words, "The love of money is the root of all evil," just as the Word of God says.

Ellen G. White writes,

> Absorbed in worldliness and pleasure seeking, the professed people of God were blinded to the Saviour's instructions concerning the signs of His appearing.... Especially was this the case in the churches of America. The freedom and comfort enjoyed by all classes of society, the ambitious desire for wealth and luxury, begetting an absorbing devotion to money-making, the eager rush for popularity and power... led men to center their interests and hopes on the things of this life. COSMIC CONFLICT, p. 274.

Freedom and comfort are both blessings of God lavished on the American people. A "young" nation has been built up from scratch by freedom-loving, hard-working people. With Christian morals as the underpinnings of social, political, and economic policies, the U.S. became a superpower and later the only superpower in the world. Prosperity and the freedom to follow the "American Dream" made America the envy of the whole world, and the hope of many to make it their home.

But *man* forgets.

God's blessings were taken for granted and forgotten. Success has been largely seen as personal achievement. Making money became an obsession in itself rather than a tool. Many lived with an "absorbing devotion to money-making." *Ibid.* For many, money became an idol.

Indulgence became a side show. "How quickly comforts can spoil a person," says Ravi Zacharias, the renowned, contemporary Christian apologist, in one of his radio messages.

Advances in technology catapulted advertising and marketing to unprecedented horizons. Consumers are forever bombarded with advertisements that only strong-minded, level-headed people can resist. With the assumption of consumption, waste became a social norm. Savings came to a halt. And credit exacerbated the imbalance.

"Nearly half of Americans would have trouble finding $400.00 to pay for an emergency," writes Neal Gabler. THE ATLANTIC, May 2016, pp. 52-63.

In 2013 the Federal Reserve Board conducted a survey to "monitor the financial and economic status of American consumers."

One of the questions asked respondents how they would pay for a $400.00 emergency.

Nearly half (47 percent) of the respondents said that "either they would cover the expense by borrowing or selling something, or they would not be able to come up with the $400.00 at all." Just four hundred dollars. And not in a developing country but in the land of plenty.

Gabler compares the prosperous 1950s and 1960s when economic growth "democratized prosperity," to the 2010s when "financial insecurity" was democratized.

Consumers carry some of the blame for the present financial insecurity. But trade and production, as well as other world economies, are major contributers.

During WWII Europe and Japan were essentially destroyed. Rebuilding in the 1950s and 1960s had been achieved through major help from the United States. America enjoyed a period of unparalleled economic growth as American factories worked at full speed and expanded to fill world-wide demand.

Foreign competition was basically nonexistent. Detroit was the car capital of the world. General Motors, Ford, and Chrysler met domestic as well as overseas demand. Prosperity was widespread.

By the 1970s Europe had resumed its industrial production, and Japan joined the competition.

In 1978 China started some economic reforms that ushered in a period of annual double-digit GDP growth. In the 1990s "President Bill Clinton signed the North American Free Trade Agreement (NAFTA) and later admitted China into the World Trade Organization (WTO)." Newt Gingrich, UNDERSTANDING TRUMP, Appendix II, Center Street, New York, Nashville, 2017, p. 322. Now China has the second-largest economy after the U.S. and Japan is in the third place.

Many believe that NAFTA and China's entry into the WTO were the most serious blows to the American economy.

President Donald Trump, in his Charlotte speech on October 26, 2016, said, "[those] two deals... de-industrialized America, uprooted our industry, and stripped bare towns like Detroit and Baltimore and the inner cities of North Carolina." UNDERSTANDING TRUMP, p. 312.

By the turn of the 21st century, the emerging markets of Brazil, Russia, India, China, and South Africa (BRICS) had come to enjoy high rates of growth, even though the rate has slowed down over the past few years. Also, South Africa is no longer included as an emerging market.

South Korea, Turkey, and Indonesia are looked upon as bright economic spots.

Great challenges are facing the American economy. High corporate taxes in America led many American manufacturers to leave the homeland and build factories overseas where labor costs are cheaper and taxes are lower. In effect, NAFTA has benefited many other countries at the expense of America.

This might explain why "financial insecurity," reported by Gabler, is now "democratized."

The increased world competition has put a downward pressure on the American trade balance. The negative impact could have been much more pronounced had it not been for the innovation and ingenuity of American entrepreneurs.

But the American consumer, voluntarily, got himself in debt. Gabler cites an analysis by the Federal Reserve and TransUnion that says: "About 38 percent of households carried some [credit card] debt,... and among those, the average was more than $15,000.00." *Ibid.*

The high interest rate charged by banks makes repayment of a $15,000.00 loan a challenge for the average family.

Neal Gabler writes,

> Maybe the 47 percent of American adults who would have trouble with a $400 emergency should have done things differently and more rationally. Maybe we all lived more grandly than we should have.... Many middle-class wage earners are victims of the economy, and, perhaps, of that... American promise... drummed into our heads since birth: Just work hard and you can have it all.

The American promise "to have it all" worked well in the era of widespread prosperity—the 1950s and 1960s. Shifting economic realities imposed some limitations on the idea. "Just work hard" has now metamorphosed into "work very hard and you can have it all."

It may well be that the generations who grew up in the prosperous years tended to trivialize the "work hard" condition and expected that "you can have it all" regardless.

"The affliction... has perhaps begun to diminish our national spirit," according to Gabler. *Ibid.* People need to feel that they are progressing, and "the lives of their children will be better than theirs."

In 2014 a <u>NEW YORK TIMES</u> poll found that "only 64 percent of Americans said they believed in the American dream....[Now] the simmering financial impotence explodes into political rage." Gabler, *Ibid.*

The cycle seems complete.

The love of money and the "ambitious desire for wealth and luxury" breed an "absorbing devotion to money-making." With that comes a sophisticated campaign of advertising and marketing to entice consumers to spend. Credit cards remove any obstacle to satisfying the appetite of shoppers. Some over spend and get themselves into trouble. Declaring bankruptcy, cheating, lying, and stealing are examples of the evil likely to emerge from "the love of money."

The Word of God says, "No man can serve two masters: for either he will hate the one, and love the other; or else he will hold to the one, and despise the other. Ye can not serve God and mammon." <u>MATTHEW</u> 6:24.

CHAPTER 4

ON CORPORATE PERFORMANCE

"A corporation is a company or group of people authorized to act as a single entity (legally a person) and recognized as such in law," according to the Wikipedia encyclopedia.

A corporation is owned by shareholders. This means that "the corporation itself, not the shareholders that own it, is held legally liable for the actions and debts the business incurs," U. S. Small Business Administration.

The previous chapter discussed the power of money on individuals. It can be a blessing or a curse (Chapter 5) depending on whether money is handled as a tool or as a goal.

Because a company or a corporation is run by individuals and because the entity has an obligation to turn a profit to its shareholders, it follows that a corporation may well fall prey to all sorts of temptations individuals experience.

Jerry Useem's article presents the case for two big corporations: Johnson & Johnson and Volkswagen, THE ATLANTIC, January/February 2016, pp. 26-28.

In 1979 James Burke, chief executive of Johnson & Johnson, summoned 20 of his key people to debate the "role of moral duties in daily business." *Ibid.*

Since 1943 the company has had a list of principles that "had been a fixture on company walls." But Burke was "worried that managers had come to regard it as... an important historical document, but hardly a tool for modern decision making." *Ibid.*

In 1982 poisoning of Tylenol capsules was a national tragedy.

Johnson & Johnson made the swift decision to remove "every bottle of Tylenol capsules from store shelves nationwide... and take a $100 million loss." *Ibid.*

When the news of poisoning broke, Burke was on a plane. "By the time he landed, employees were already ordering Tylenol off store shelves."

Volkswagen, by contrast, "seems intent on poisoning its own product, name, and future." Is it conceivable to unconsciously install a "defeat device" into hundreds of thousands of cars? "You need to be sneaky, and thus deliberate." *Ibid.*

Useem describes how corporate culture may change over time. He notes examples where decisions at the top did have detrimental consequences. Ford, Pinto, NASA Challenger, and B. F. Goodrich aircraft brake all went through a sequence of events that "appears and reappears in corporate misconduct cases, beginning with the fantastic commitments made from on high." *Ibid.*

In the early 1970s Denny Gioia was coordinator of product recalls at Ford Motor Company. At the time the Pinto tended to explode when hit from behind. But a "set of unwritten scripts imported from the organization around them," helped managers make decisions, and eased the cognitive load generated by bombardment with information. Scripts can be flawed, and "grow more so over time, yet they discourage active analysis." *Ibid.*

Gioia felt "no strong obligation" to recall.

Seventeen years after he had left the company, he wrote, "I now argue and teach [at Penn State] that Ford had an ethical obligation to recall. But, while I was there... remember no strong ethical overtones to the case whatsoever." *Ibid.*

At NASA it was the O-rings. Morton-Thiokol contracted with NASA to design the O-rings. Engineers at Morton-Thiokol "noticed O-ring damage that looked different from damage they'd seen before." *Ibid.*

Cold was suspected as a factor in causing the damage noticed on the previous space shuttle.

The "near-freezing forecast" on the evening of the fatal Challenger launch led engineers to make a 'no launch' recommendation. They faxed the data to NASA to support their view. But the data were the same as those "they had earlier used to argue that the space shuttle was safe to fly." *Ibid.*

Top management at Morton-Thiokol felt embarrassed and could not "overturn the script they themselves had built in the preceding years.... The "no launch" recommendation was reversed to 'launch.'" *Ibid.*

In 1968 B. F. Goodrich built for the Air Force an aircraft brake that "many employees *knew* would fail." The prototype was first tried at the company's test laboratory. It overheated and "spewed incendiary bits of metal." *Ibid.*

A young engineer discovered that the brake design put forward by a senior engineer was wrong. In the meantime, brake components from other suppliers were being delivered. Redesigning the brake would "wreck the promised timetable."

Testing continued. The brake should have withstood 50 simulated landings. To deal with the overheating, "fans were brought in for cooling. Warped components were machined back into shape between stops." *Ibid.* Despite all the efforts made to nurse the brake through the repeated landings, success proved elusive.

Kermit Vandivier, the data analyst at the test lab, and several colleagues were "told to prepare a report showing that the brake qualified." *Ibid.*

Vandivier agonized for a month between becoming a party to the fraud or refusing and losing his job. He "resigned and became a newspaper reporter."

Back to Volkswagen's scandal. Jerry Useem writes that in 2008 a corruption trial sent a company executive to jail. Ferdinand Piech, VW's chairman, referred to "alleged widespread use of VW funds on prostitutes as mere 'irregularities,' .... This was around the time the emissions cheating began." *Ibid.*

> Culture starts at the top.... But it does not start at the top with pretty statements. Employees will see through empty rhetoric and will emulate the nature of top-management decision making. *Ibid.*

On November 19, 2016 Volkswagen announced that it would lay off 30,000 jobs because of the emission scandal. On January 13, 2017 it was reported that VW would pay a $4.3 billion fine and six employees were indicted. All the six were German citizens. Only Oliver Schmidt, 48, was arrested in Miami while on vacation and "held without bail until trial." NORTHWEST FLORIDA DAILY NEWS, January 13, 2017, p. A6.

A drug manufacturing company proved not immune from money temptations. In 2008 Daiichi Sankyo of Japan paid "$4.6 billion for a 64 percent stake" in Ranbaxy, an Indian firm that "looked like a rising star... in generic medicines." THE ECONOMIST, September 21, 2013, p. 65.

Since then Ranbaxy suffered some safety problems that were called to the attention of American regulators. The firm's new plant at Mohali in Punjab "was supposed to solve Ranbaxy's quality problems." But FDA inspectors "found fault with its manufacturing processes," and had to impose a ban on medicines from the new plant. This marks the FDA's "third ban on a Ranbaxy plant in five years." *Ibid.*

The company's troubles actually started even before building the new factory in Mohali.

Ranbaxy agreed to pay $500 million to settle its case with the U. S. Department of Justice after admitting that, among other things, "it had *invented* safety data for some of its medicines." *Ibid.*

In 2012 Ranbaxy sales in America (where it has a factory) exceeded $1 billion which accounted for about half of its total revenues.

The director of project and information management joined Ranbaxy in 2003. He resigned in 2005 after he discovered the firm's practices and informed American regulators.

Ranbaxy was "charged in a legal case in 2007, [that it] had *invented* data to win approval for drugs in America and for treatments for HIV patients around the world." *Ibid.*

As the Word says, "The love of money is the root of all evil."

Countrywide Financial was a "leading originator of sub prime mortgage loans." THE ECONOMIST, September 28, 2013, p. 67. Two government-sponsored housing-finance giants, Fannie Mae and Freddie Mac, "bought vast amounts of these mortgages." All three institutions imploded.

The Bank of America agreed to buy the failing Countrywide for $4 billion in 2008. The Bank of America "found itself the proud owner of a giant legal cesspool." *Ibid.*

At the trial of the Bank of America, Rebecca Mairone, a mid-tier executive who worked at Countrywide for only two-and-a-half years, was a co-defendant.

It turned out that Countrywide's "rise and fall came under the leadership of Angelo Mozilo, whose managerial style included running a 'friends of Angelo' list that handed loans at favorable rates to politicians." Mozilo and two other company executives settled legal claims back in 2010 "without admitting or denying guilt." I*bid.*

The prosecution went after the automated loan-processing system that Countrywide used to point out "what appeared to be" credit worthy borrowers. The system was called the "high-speed swim lane" or HSSL. *Ibid.*

In order to qualify for this HSSL, you do not need to know how to swim.

As has been the case with Volkswagen (defeat devices), Ford (Pinto explosions), B. F. Goodrich (failing aircraft brakes), Morton-Thiokol (damaged O-rings), Ranbaxy (invented safety data), or Countrywide (sub prime mortgage loans extended to borrowers using the HSSL system), the problem usually starts at top management and slowly spreads downward to dominate the organizational culture. The unwritten goal is to make more profit, meet promised deadlines, or gain favor with the powerful. All seem to fall under the category of the "love of money."

It may be argued that CEOs are under pressure from shareholders to turn in a profit. Quarterly earnings tend to overshadow long-term investment policies. Competition, intensified by globalization initiated by NAFTA, is making decision making even tougher at the top.

Beside shareholders, CEOs are coming under more scrutiny from corporate boards. "For most of their history, boards have been largely ceremonial institutions: friends of the boss who meet every few months to rubber-stamp his decisions and have a good lunch," writes Schumpeter. THE ECONOMIST, December 7, 2013, p. 72.

But this is changing. In the 2000s some "corporate scandals [have] forced boards to take a more active role." *Ibid.*

Ram Charan, Den nis Carey, and Michael Useem opine in their book that boards are becoming strategic partners BOARDS THAT LEAD. To guard against creating "warring centers of power," Charan and his co-authors outline two rules.

First, boards "should focus on providing companies with strategic advice...." The authors say that in their experience perhaps half of the

Fortune 500 companies have one or two directors they would regard as "dysfunctional." *Ibid.*

The second rule is for the boards to get "their relationship with the CEO right.... They need to act as personal mentors... giving the boss frank advice." *Ibid.*

Schumpeter wonders whether directors can monitor performance while simultaneously being "responsible for helping to set strategy and appointing the CEO.... Will CEOs willingly give up more power to boards, or will they fight back?" *Ibid.* All are legitimate concerns in a fast-paced world.

The corporate world has always been at the heart of capitalism. Its performance signaled whether or not and where to invest.

To "measure" performance, auditors are hired. External auditors should be better suited to provide an accurate, unbiased assessment. Or at least, this was the thinking.

After the most recent financial meltdown, "calls to reform accounting have grown particularly loud," THE ECONOMIST, December 7, 2013, p. 68. Both America and the European Union are working on introducing "new rules aimed at enhancing auditors' independence," to ensure that advertised ratings are not overblown.

The European Commission is expected to require "mandatory audit rotation... to require firms to put their audits out for tender once a decade and to change auditors every 20 years." *Ibid.* Mandatory audit rotation was absent from the American proposals.

The case for rotation is that "auditors who keep the same client for too long get excessively cozy with its management." *Ibid.*

Not surprisingly, accounting giants oppose change. They finance academic research to prove their view. Tobacco companies also financed research to prove that smoking is *not* addictive.

"Auditors have a conflict of interest at the heart of their business—they are paid by the companies they are supposed to assess objectively." *Ibid.*

Cozy relationships between corporate management and the auditors may not be the sole source of public outcry.

Collusion between employees at major banks has also been brought to light. "The widening scandal over fixing of benchmark interest rates such as LIBOR,... could encourage a race to own up by firms involved in gaming other benchmarks, including exchange rates," THE ECONOMIST, December 7, 2013, p. 79.

Five financial institutions agreed to pay $2.3 billion to the European Commission. These included Deutsche Bank, Societe Generale, Royal Bank of Scotland, JP Morgan Chase, and Citigroup.

"The Commission also offered immunity to banks that blew the whistle on the cartel." *Ibid.*

All the darkness can not extinguish a candle's light.

"UBS avoided a $3.4 billion fine and Barclay's a $930 million one for their part in rigging rates because they confessed early." *Ibid.*

All were guilty, but a few were smarter and confessed earlier.

And the scandals continued. In 2016 THE WALL STREET JOURNAL, December 19, p. B8, reported that Deutsche Bank was "negotiating with the Justice Department to resolve claims over mortgage securities it sold in the run-up to the financial crisis." In September 2016 Deutsche Bank "rejected a $14 billion settlement offer from the government."

The allure of money could not stop some well-paid executives at major financial institutions from committing crime. Highly compensated auditors had no qualms about inflating ratings for firms or financial instruments they knew were losing money.

It is no wonder that the Word of God warns us of the "love" of money.

ECONOMICS

Thomas Carlyle, the 19th century polemicist, mocked the discipline as "the dismal science," THE ECONOMIST, November 23, 2013, p. 58. Economists "not only failed to spot the precipice [the 2008 nightmare], many forecast exactly the opposite—a tranquil stability they called 'the great moderation.'"

The 2013 Nobel prize winners in economics were Eugene Fama of Chicago, Robert Shiller from Yale, and Lars Peter Hansen (also of Chicago).

Fama has an "ardent belief in the efficiency of markets."

Shiller, in contrast, "is known for his prescient warnings of bubbles, in technology stocks in the 1990s and in housing in the 2000s."

The three laureates "disagree with one another about how markets operate... [they] have established most of the surprisingly small amount economics has to say about asset prices." *Ibid.*

What the three accomplished economists agree about is to "back up theoretical work with rigorous empirical analysis." *Ibid.*

Shortly after being informed of his award, Hansen "was asked how well economists are doing in understanding asset prices." He answered, "We are making a little bit of progress, but there is a lot more to be done." *Ibid.*

Looking at economics from another angle reveals how the "prize in economic sciences in memory of Alfred Nobel, as it is officially known, sometimes struggles to command the same respect as its counterparts" in physics, chemistry, and medicine. The Nobel prize in economics was a "latecomer to the ceremonies, established in 1968 by Sweden's central bank rather than in 1896 by Mr. Nobel's will." *Ibid.*

Students of economics are "eager to learn what went wrong [to cause the financial crisis of 2008], but frustrated by what they are taught." *Ibid.* Some new projects aim to address this.

In the early 1930s the global economy was "stuck in a rut, and economists could not explain why." In 1933 John Maynard Keynes of Cambridge introduced a new theory. He explained "how deficient demand could lead to persistent recessions and long-term unemployment." *Ibid.*

Keynes's ideas became widely accepted after John Hicks of Cambridge "distilled them into a simple model which quickly became the backbone of undergraduate teaching." *Ibid.*

In Britain many university students of economics are disappointed by what they study. Among their demands are "fewer lectures bogged down in detailed mathematics, and more time discussing important historical thinkers." *Ibid.*

In a letter to the editor, Marco Schneebalg writes regarding rethinking economics,

> We would also like to see a greater exposure of students to different schools of economic thought; a closer integration of economics with other social sciences; and a greater awareness of the inherent fallibility of economics, that all its findings are contingent on the institutions and culture of a given time and place, <u>THE ECONOMIST</u>, December 7, 2013, p. 18.

Schneebalg is correct in emphasizing the fallibility of economics and its dependence on "institutions and culture of a given time and place." Could this explain why Thomas Carlyle referred to economics as "the dismal science?"

For economics to be contingent on "institutions and culture of a given time and place" does not reconcile well with the long-agreed-upon principles of science.

CHAPTER 5

AS A CURSE

Walter White, the hero of the television series "Breaking Bad," is a high school chemistry teacher with a second job at a car wash. Out of the blue, he was told that he has cancer. To cover his cancer treatment and "leave his family a nest egg" after passing away, he decides to go into the "highly lucrative methamphetamine business." Schumpeter, THE ECONOMIST, September 28, 2013, p. 64.

The popular television series is "one of the best studies available of the dynamics of modern business." Among other things it evinces the "breakdown of relations between business partners, thanks to the acids of ego, greed, and paranoia, is a perennial business problem.... Strained relations between companies and distributors are common." *Ibid.*

Ego and greed feed a set of illusions. The more successful the person becomes, the more invulnerable s/he feels. "The more rules he breaks, the more righteous he feels. And the more wealth he accumulates, the more he wants." *Ibid.*

As Dr. Charles Stanley said, "We are created with a void that only God can fill."

From 2003–2005 Jose Dirceu was the chief of staff of President Luiz Inacio Lula da Silva of Brazil. This made him the second most powerful man in the country.

In this South American country "impunity for politicians has long been the norm." THE ECONOMIST, November 23, 2013, p. 39. Few Brazilians believed that Dirceu "would be charged, let alone convicted or jailed."

But on November 15, 2013 the Supreme Court issued warrants for his arrest together with 11 others "among the 25 found guilty last year of, variously, bribery, money-laundering, misuse of public funds, and conspiracy." *Ibid.*

Drug trafficking has a powerful allure. Cultivated in South America, drugs find their way to their wealthy neighbor to the north. (This is part of the reason why we need a wall, primarily to stop the flow of the "poison.")

President Richard Nixon started the war on drugs in 1971. For the first 20 years, "Mexican traffickers were a footnote, little more than border smugglers for Pablo Escobar, the Colombian billionaire drug trafficker." *Ibid.*

In 1989 Escobar attempted to kill a Colombian presidential candidate by orchestrating the bombing of a commercial airliner. Two Americans happened to be on board.

"That put Escobar in the cross hairs of the U. S. military. Four years later he was gunned down." David Epstein, THE ATLANTIC, January/February, 2016, pp. 78-92.

When the U. S. Navy blocked smuggling routes to Florida, the traffickers spread allover the Mexican border.

The vacuum Escobar left behind allowed a "cadre of ambitious Mexican criminals" to step in. *Ibid.*

One of them was Benjamin Arellano Felix. He was the second oldest of seven brothers and became the first head of the Arellano Felix Organization (AFO).

"By the early 1990s, the cartel was smuggling in 40 percent of the cocaine consumed in the United States." The Arellano brothers "controlled the flow of drugs through... the single most important point for illicit commerce in the world: the border crossing from Tijuana to San Diego." *Ibid.*

In 2005 Javier Arellano Felix, the youngest of the Arellano brothers, was the head of the AFO. The Drug Enforcement Agency (DEA) launched Operation Shadow Game designed to follow Javier. In August 2006 the DEA boarded Dock Holiday, the 43-foot yacht bought earlier by the AFO, that raised suspicions of the American authorities.

"Javier's arrest would be hailed by officials in the States as a decisive victory in what may have been the longest active case in the DEA's history." *Ibid.*

The agency's chief of operations announced, "We feel like we've taken the head off the snake." *Ibid.* This was reason for celebration was it not for the sad reality that it was an octopus rather than a snake. And the saga continues.

The Arellano brothers were brutal. Ramon, the fifth of the seven brothers, was considered the "most ruthless killer in Mexico." Their first line of defense was not their own men but Mexico's law enforcement. "Mexican officials' corruption was not a matter of if, but when," David Epstein was told by the DEA's agent assigned to the case. "Certain military generals made $250,000 a month. Prosecutors were paid a la carte." *Ibid.*

Through the 1980s the Arellano brothers tolerated Chapo Guzman. Money, inventory, and turf were abundant to "accommodate every criminal appetite." *Ibid.* But in 1989 Ramon killed a man who had assaulted his sister years earlier. The man was a close friend of Guzman.

Shortly afterwards, the brothers "declared all of Baja, California their territory." *Ibid.* Obviously, Chapo was not very happy.

"Guzman started digging the Sinaloa cartel's first known drug-smuggling tunnel under AFO turf." *Ibid.* He made plans to kill the seven Arellano brothers.

In May 1993 Ramon and a dozen of his men went to Guadalajara to kill Chapo Guzman. They failed to find Guzman and decided to fly back to Tijuana.

Suddenly, Guzman was spotted at the airport. A firefight erupted. AFO people "poured bullets into a white Grand Marquis, killing the driver and a passenger." *Ibid.* It turned out later that the passenger was Cardinal Juan Jesus Posadas Ocampo, the second-highest-ranking official in Mexico's Roman Catholic Church.

"Guzman fled to Guatemala, where he was arrested two weeks later." In prison he "enjoyed chess, basketball,... and the bands he brought in to perform." *Ibid.* Chapo continued to run his drug business.

The Arellano brothers sent $10 million and two gang members to give false confessions to the director of the Mexican Federal Judicial Police. Authorities bought the brothers time by "raiding houses that the cartel had already abandoned." *Ibid.* The AFO scattered.

The Cardinal's murder brought the AFO case to the forefront of the American authorities. Luckily, one day in 1995 the DEA got some invaluable information from an insider who "was ready to spill AFO secrets." *Ibid.*

The insider told that "pickup trucks with false beds were being delivered to... [a] home in La Jolla, each loaded with a ton of cocaine." *Ibid.* The DEA also got the name of the Arellano brothers' top lieutenant in Tijuana, a piece of information that had eluded them.

Just like the case with Islamic jihadists, as authorities take out a "leader," others jump in to fill the vacuum.

After the killing of the Cardinal, Ramon Arellano had to lie low. "In his absence, the rank and file got sloppy." *Ibid.* A series of missteps drew the attention of the Mexican military. When Ramon was added to the FBI's "Ten Most Wanted" list in September 1997, he fled from Los Angeles to Mexico.

With the return of Ramon to Mexico, "the Arellano brothers reassembled. They were still dominant in Tijuana, but the Sinaloa cartel was gaining strength." *Ibid.*

An informant told the FBI "the location of Eduardo Arellano's new house in Tijuana. A corrupt Mexican police chief tipped Eduardo off and he fled with his wife... and their two children to a safe house." *Ibid.*

Eduardo's wife, Sonia, had to use a propane tank for cooking because the safe house was "not quite ready to be lived in." One night the propane tank was accidentally left open until morning. When Sonia struck a match to make breakfast, the house exploded. "The baby in her arms went flying and was critically injured... [her] face melted into a welter of raw flesh and blisters." *Ibid.*

As stated earlier, money can be a curse because the love of money is the root of all evil.

AFO's top lieutenant in Tijuana, Kitty Paez, had been arrested earlier and was "becoming the first Mexican drug trafficker extradited to the U. S." *Ibid.*

Fast forward to 2006. The arrest of Javier Arellano was "the cartel's death knell." *Ibid.*

Eduardo was the last of the brothers who was alive, free, and "had any experience leading the cartel." *Ibid.* One of his confidants gave him up. In 2008 he was arrested in his home in Tijuana.

The eldest brother, Francisco, was "the last to meet his fate. He was at his 64th birthday party... when a man dressed as a clown walked in, shot him dead, and walked out." *Ibid.*

It took two decades of well-concerted efforts by the authorities to have every one of the Arellano brothers either dead or behind bars. But it certainly was worthwhile. The damage they did was immeasurable. The Arellano brothers were "shipping up to 40,000 pounds of cocaine each month to just one distributor in Los Angeles." *Ibid.*

81

The flip side of the government's achievement is that the war on drugs does not seem to be working. "There are more drugs coming across the border than ever," an agent familiar with the case tells David Epstein. *Ibid.*

> While the cocaine trade has plunged in the United States in recent years, the heroin and methamphetamine markets have exploded. The amount of meth seized at the southwest border has more than quintupled since 2008, and the amount of heroin has more than tripled.

That is probably why David Epstein titled his article in THE ATLANTIC "Unfinished Business."

The drug trafficking business continues to attract many seeking the "big bucks." Most will perish before they have the chance to realize that it is *cursed* money.

A CULTURE OF DEPENDENCE

Money can be a curse other than in the drug business.

A parent may harm his/her child by providing money in a way that over time conveys a message that dissociates money from work. The youngster grows up thinking that money comes easily without much effort or sacrifice.

Evan Thomas, NEWSWEEK, March 8, 2010, p. 27 writes,

> The problem is not the system. It is us—our "get mine" culture of entitlement. It is hard to know exactly how or when we got this self-indulgent.... The... explosion of free expression contributed to the sour and selfish "Me Decade" of the 1970s. The spurt of economic activity in the 1980s and 90s spawned a generation of... profligate spenders in the shopping malls of America.

George F. Will, <u>NEWSWEEK</u>, March 8, 2010, p. 24 talks about "The Basement Boys." He quotes Gary Cross, a Pennsylvania State University historian, who cites a recent study that found that 55 percent of men between the ages of 18 and 24 are living in their parents' homes as are 13 percent of men between 25 and 34.

Quoting Gary Cross, George Will says that the "culture of the boy-men today is less a life stage than a life style…. Permissive parenting made children less submissive, and the decline of deference coincided with the rise of consumer and media cultures celebrating the indefinite retention of the tastes and habits of childhood." *Ibid.*

From another perspective the availability of easy money has created a chronic social problem. Instead of just having the parents spoiling their children by acting as negative role models, some government policies, unintentionally, helped to fortify the mentality of dependence by expanding social assistance programs.

In principle a safety net provides protection for the physically- and/or mentally-challenged citizens.

Abusers always find a way to beat the system. Loopholes are an inherent reality in man-made laws. Over time, abuse has the power to convert a noble idea into a national liability.

The welfare system provides subsidies that cover almost all aspects of life: food stamps, subsidized housing, help with energy and utility bills, education and childcare assistance, health care and medical provisions, cash assistance, as well as subsidies and assistance for other basic services.

A married couple may not qualify for assistance if they both have incomes—a common occurrence in our times. To qualify they have to divorce or one of them has to quit work. One option destroys the family while the other lowers the family's standard of living.

But with the welfare system now in place, that family would get more money if they divorce or one of them quits working. Money comes from the government coffers to pay someone for doing nothing.

Dave Hodges, "THE COMMON SENSE SHOW", says, "The next time you go into the DMV,... you are subsidizing a driver's license for a third of the people. You are also paying for their health care, food stamps, and shelter. And many of these... poverty-stricken 'Americans' are living a higher standard of living than you are.... Gary Alexander, Secretary of Public Welfare, Pennsylvania, explained over two years ago that 'the single mom is better off earning a gross income of $29,000 with $57,327 in net income and benefits than earning a gross income of $69,000 with net income and benefits of $57,045.'"

An unmarried female with one child soon comes to realize that having more children translates into more assistance and subsidies.

The children grow up amid an environment void of self reliance, work ethics, and even self respect. And the cycle of dependence continues.

With a national debt that is around $20 trillion in 2017, one has to wonder how long our country can afford this situation.

Instead of being a blessing, money can be a curse for the individual as well as for society.

PART III

PART III: POWER OF CONTROL

God created man. He gave *man* authority over creatures in the sea, the air, and over all the earth.

A loving God is pleased with man's worship and fellowship, but He still dignifies humanity by never forcing Himself on anyone. He "knocks" at the door of man's heart. The created chooses whether or not to allow the Creator into his/her life.

Vertically, *man* enjoys freedom in his relationship with a merciful, graceful God.

Horizontally, *man's* relationship with others is a lot more complicated.

The tendency to control is an inherent human impulse.

Democratic institutions limit the phenomenon by creating checks and balances.

CEOs have almost a free hand in running their corporations. However, this has been changing after some detrimental decisions failed to invite serious review by the board of directors.

Communist and socialist regimes offer a panorama of the control of *man* by fellow *man*.

CHAPTER 6

CONTROL OF NATIONS

"China and Vietnam have two of the few Communist Parties still in power." Banyan, THE ECONOMIST, October 26, 2013, p. 52. It is therefore not surprising that both have to deal with similar problems.

In Vietnam the Communist Party Central Committee scheduled meetings in the autumn of 2013 to debate proposed changes to the country's constitution.

"The current version, adopted in 1992... no longer reflects the more open economy and society that Vietnam has become." *Ibid.*

Reformers hope that the constitution might provide guarantees for an independent judiciary. An existing article states that the Communist Party is "the force leading the state and society" in a one-party system. Another article declares that "the state's economic sector shall play the leading role in the national economy." *Ibid.* The profligacy of Vietnam's state-owned enterprises is partly responsible for the country's debt crisis.

"One party, the Communist Party, controls the economic, social, and political activities in a country of more than 90 million people." ECONOMIST INTELLIGENCE UNIT, "The World in 2013," p. 114.

Would Vietnam be able to dismantle the state's economic sector? Perhaps. But doing so is "terrifying for many. Not only are officials corrupt beneficiaries of business links. The system also helps to justify single-party rule." *Ibid.*

In China, the Communist Party critics "want it simply to respect the present constitution." It promises "equality, freedoms of speech, assembly and religion, and an independent judiciary, all of which the Communist Party ignores." *Ibid.*

As of 2013, the Chinese Communist Party controls the social, economic, and political life of 1.34 billion people—as of 2013.

But *man's* appetite for control can hardly be satisfied. Only the presence of the Holy Spirit can restrain *man's* wild instincts.

Tibet is an autonomous region of China. Jokhang Temple is Tibet's spiritual heart, revered for its golden statue of the young Buddha. GOOGLE.

From 2011 to 2013 "more than 120 Tibetans have set fire to themselves in protest." Banyan, THE ECONOMIST, December 7, 2013, p. 48.

In 2013 nine Tibetans were sentenced for alleged separatist activity. In spite of expanding freedoms for the majority in China, "dissidents are still persecuted." Liu Xiaobo, winner of the 2010 Nobel Peace Prize, "remains in jail for no more than advocating peaceful, incremental political reform." *Ibid.*

Control and freedom are mutually exclusive.

The Communist Party likes to make life difficult for foreign journalists. Authorities "have halted the annual visa-renewal process for at least two dozen journalists working for American media, after they wrote stories about the wealth accumulated by the families of China's leaders." THE ECONOMIST, December 14, 2013, p. 54.

By definition, single-party systems exert total control of a nation. The proclaimed ideology that justifies one-party rule is probably less of an ideology than an exercise in control disguised as philosophical principles.

It is not only the Communist Party that has a monopoly on power. Many authoritative regimes exert control by restrictive policies that limit freedom of speech, human rights, the press, and any sign of dissent.

From countries in Africa, South America, and Asia strong rulers enjoy total authority. They govern countries of different cultures, languages, religions, and history. But the common factor is the temptation for total dominance.

Religion and ethnicity may mask the inner tendencies for power, dominance, and control. Southeast Asia offers a rather recent illustration.

In 1947 a bloody war had led to the partition of India. Pakistan was created. It was made up of two parts: west and east, one thousand miles apart, divided by hostile Indian territory. Both parts of Pakistan are Muslim dominated.

The western part achieved dominance. "It had the capital Islamabad, and greater political, economic and military clout." The Pashtuns were better worriors and the Punjabis were more prosperous. They "looked down on Bengali easterners as passive and backward." THE BIRTH OF BENGLADESH, THE ECONOMIST, September 21, 2013, pp. 90-91.

In 1971 Pakistan split into two countries, and Bangladesh was born. The split was perhaps inevitable. It happened following Pakistan's first national election, late in 1970, that brought a shock to West Pakistanis.

> an easterner, Sheikh Mujibur Rahman, won a sweeping victory, and was poised to lead the country. His Awami League wanted greater rights for Bengalis. But the army chiefs and politicians in Islamabad would not countenance his taking office. They arrested him and the army began repressing eastern protesters. *Ibid.*

Muslim citizens of West Pakistan could not tolerate receding power to Muslims of East Pakistan. Shared culture and religion took second place to the appetite for control.

As the army began a campaign of persecuting East Pakistanis, the "Bengalis flocked to join the rebel forces who were fighting for independence." *Ibid.*

Pakistani soldiers stationed in East Pakistan started "targeting students, writers, politicians; especially the Hindu minority." Army soldiers burned villages and massacred civilians. Millions fled to India. Some 10 million East Pakistanis became refugees, most of them were Hindus. It was reported that 300,000 people were killed, but "some say the death toll was over one million." *Ibid.*

Gary Bass, a Princeton academic, argues that the "killings amounted to a genocide." Hindus in East Pakistan were a distinct minority. They were "chosen for annihilation and expulsion."

In 1971 India intervened in the war that had been going on in East Pakistan. After supporting East Pakistan's rebels for months, India's army "crushed the Pakistani forces within days."

Pakistan was humiliated. Pakistanis thought that India might next "try to break up the remaining western rump of their country." *Ibid.* Sharp suspicion still lingers to this day between India and Pakistan.

Nor did the war help India. Refugees returned to their homes, but relations between India and Bangladesh "soon soured." Gandhi, the Prime Minister of India, descended into authoritarianism and suspended democracy.

In Bangladesh "the war remains a live political issue as alleged collaborators in the conflict... are being tried by a flawed, local war-crimes tribunal." *Ibid.*

Hundreds of thousands of people were killed in a war essentially instigated by inherent tendency for control.

In Africa, Sudan went through a civil war that went on for years costing the lives of a million people. Ethnic Arab tribes fought with black Africans. Reaching a stage of genocide of Christians by fanatic Muslims led to the establishment of a new country by splitting Sudan into two nations. South Sudan became an independent state where Christians enjoy autonomous rule separate from the Muslim-majority north.

Across time and geography, dominance by control is indelible. It is evident in a myriad of countries and political systems.

"China's communist rulers see the deaths on Tia-nanmen Square in 1989 as blood well spilled," <u>THE ECONOMIST</u>, September 28, 2013, pp. 56-57. In 2009 many protesters were killed in Iran by the Mullah's regime. Bashar El Assid may "feel that his atrocities in Syria have been vindicated."

For almost thirty years Saddam Hussein's brutal rule of Iraq had seen the use of chemical weapons and executions of both the Shia majority as well as the minority Kurds. The demise of his Sunni regime in 2003 gave rise to widespread unrest as a backlash of the Shias against the Sunnis.

Muammar Qaddafi lasted for more than 40 years as the absolute ruler of Libya.

His policy was to turn tribes against each other. He did not trust Libyans with his personal security and relied instead on African body guards from Chad, an adjacent country.

The "Arab Spring" of 2011, first in Tunisia then in Egypt, spread to Libya. Within a few months rebels took control and eventually captured the dictator who was bludgeoned to death.

Not all dictators end up being killed. "The first risk for despots is that a crackdown may flop: troops and goons can not or will not always enact emergency laws or obey orders to shoot." *Ibid.*

In the Philippines, security forces became disobedient and helped finish Ferdinand Marcos's rule. The same happened in Siberia to Slobodan Milosevic.

Even when orders are obeyed, "repression can ultimately strengthen the opposition," as John Steinbeck wrote. In the end, brutality can backfire, and "harsh repression shortens leaders' tenure." *Ibid.*

Suharto, the late president of Indonesia, abused the separatists in Aceh. "An onslaught in 1989 suppressed the rebellion—only for it to flare up, with broader support, a decade later." *Ibid.*

In 1905 Russian demonstrators were killed in large enough numbers to cause resentment that "helped to doom Tsar Nicholas II 13 years later." *Ibid.*

And it is not only the autocrats who are tempted by violence and control. Britain's General Reginald Dyer was "responsible for killing hundreds of Indians at Amritsar in 1919." *Ibid.*

Whereas temptation for control may be disguised as being for the common good, repression does not always work.

"History suggests that... violence is counterproductive: those that turn the other cheek, opting for civil disobedience, sit-ins, and strikes rather than armed retaliation, tend to do best." *Ibid.*

Erica Chenoweth of the University of Denver and Maria Stephan of the U.S. State Department "analyzed protests designed to remove governments... between 1900 and 2006.... They concluded [that] peaceful uprisings are twice as likely to succeed as violent ones."

The infallibility of God's Word is proven even through "protests." Peaceful protesters—those who turn the other cheek to violent authorities—are "twice as likely to succeed as violent ones." *Ibid.*

CHAPTER 7

CONTROL OF
CORPORATIONS

In the competitive world of capitalism, corporations are an integral part. Their success and prosperity are reflected in society bringing more jobs to people who consume products made available by other corporations. The cycle continues maintaining a healthy GDP growth of three percentage points or more.

By the same token, wrong decisions can be detrimental. The "defeat devices" of Volkswagen, Ford Pinto, NASA Challenger, and B. F. Goodrich aircraft brake systems are some examples of "corporate misconduct cases, beginning with the fantastic commitments made from on high," as pointed out earlier in CHAPTER 4.

Schumpeter writes about Paul Flowers, the former chairman of Britain's Cooperative Bank and a Methodist minister, who "allegedly bought cocaine and crystal meth for a 'drug-fueled' orgy." THE ECONOMIST, November 30, 2013, p. 67.

Rob Ford, Toronto's mayor "has finally admitted, after months of denials, that he smoked crack cocaine—before adding the comforting proviso that he only did it in 'one of my drunken stupors.'" *Ibid.*

Schumpeter notes that chief executives are under tremendous pressure to perform, turning the corner office almost into "a factory for personal problems." *Ibid.*

The challenges are greater in periods of economic turmoil. The power bestowed on the CEO can be corruptive.

Experiments by social scientists have shown, "by giving random subjects power over others, that even in small doses it produces overconfidence, insensitivity and an urge to associate with other people with power." *Ibid.*

To put it differently, power exposes the innate human tendency for control that is sometimes accompanied by negative practices.

"Chief executives' oddities can lead to complete corporate breakdown," such as what happened at World.com or Hollinger, or the Royal Bank of Scotland. But even in less dysfunctional firms "the whims of the man at the top can cause damaging depression... below. Chief executives are the nearest things democracies have to sun kings." *Ibid.*

THE ECONOMIST article points out three signs of a boss "breaking bad." The first sign is grandiosity. "He attributes the company's success wholly to himself, indulges in endless self-promotion or demands ever more extravagant rewards." *Ibid.*

A second sign is over control. "The boss surrounds himself with yes-men and crushes dissent." *Ibid.* What a repressive regime imposes on a nation, the CEO follows in running a corporation.

The third sign is "distorted decision making. The chief conflates personal and corporate assets, and is obsessed with buying other companies." *Ibid.*

The longer a chief executive stays at the job, the likelier he may "succumb to these vanities." The encouraging sign is that CEOs "last half as long in the job, on average, as they did a decade ago... [this] makes them less likely to become marinated in power." *Ibid.*

Just as corporations are at the heart of capitalism, start-ups supply the blood stream that keeps it functioning and growing. "Start-ups have always been at the heart of America's economic success." THE ECONOMIST, October 12, 2013, p. 78. They account for most of the innovations that have made America the bastion of new discoveries.

"Established firms are usually in the business of preserving the old world," putting more pressure on start-ups to come up with new ideas. If successful, they usually create a lot of new jobs. "But these growth machines have broken down.... Start-ups created 2.7 million new jobs in... 2012... compared with 4.7 million in 1999." *Ibid.*

In 2010 John Dearie and Courtney Geduldig published a book titled WHERE THE JOBS ARE in which they try to explain the "parlous state" of entrepreneurship. The authors identify four areas of concern. *Ibid.*

The first is the "human capital." Universities are "failing to keep pace with a fast-changing job market." *Ibid.* Small firms are unable to provide the appropriate training and consequently employ fewer people but let them work longer hours.

Tied to the first concern is our immigration policy. Countries send their best and brightest to the U.S. to get their post-graduate degrees. But after 9/11, most foreign students must leave the U. S. The negative impact is ineffable. "Immigrants are responsible for launching about half the country's most successful start-ups and producing a striking number of its patents." *Ibid.*

Max Marty is raising money to "moor a ship in international waters off San Francisco. Foreign-born entrepreneurs will work in the floating office-park and make trips to Silicon Valley." *Ibid.* The innovative idea is expensive but cost-benefit analysis apparently lends it credit.

Regulations and taxes are the source of complaints by entrepreneurs. From 2009 to 2011 the Obama administration "issued 106 new regulations each expected to have an economic impact of at least $100 million a year." In addition, investors suffer from an environment of uncertainty brought about by new legislation, for example, Obamacare and "ideological trench warfare." *Ibid.*

The Vanguard Group estimates that from 2011 to 2013 "bickering politicians have imposed, in effect, a $261 billion uncertainty tax," costing one million new jobs. *Ibid.*

America previously imposed a 35 percent corporate tax that was considered to be among the highest in the world. The Trump administration has reduced it to 21 percent.

Raising money is another area of concern. More than "70 percent of new businesses are launched using savings or assets—particularly houses." The financial crisis has reduced the "average net worth of American households by about 40 percent." *Ibid.*

The challenges facing start-ups are compounded by the ability of established firms to exercise what Schumpeter terms "talent wars," THE ECONOMIST, December 14, 2013, p. 76. "eBay pays its lead technologist twice as much as its chief executive. Apple recently slipped a high-flyer $8 million to prevent him from jumping ship."

Talent wars are also fought with lawsuits and handcuffs. "Corporations are increasingly resorting to litigation... to prevent employees from moving to rivals," thus clogging the labor market. *Ibid.*

In the arena of employee control, the "non-compete" agreement prevents employees "leaving a firm from working for a rival for a fixed period... or setting up a competing business." *Ibid.* It is estimated that now 90 percent of managerial and technical employees in America have signed that agreement.

Other weapons are available for corporations to control their employees. "Companies can prevent former workers... from moving to a rival on the grounds that they are taking trade secrets with them." This falls under the "confidential information" and "pre-invention assignment" requirements signed at employment. *Ibid.*

CHAPTER 8

POLITICAL POWER

A softer, gentler form of control is that of political parties. In America two political parties share the honor. Their control of power is not as absolute as that of the Communist Party (CHAPTER 6) or that of corporations (CHAPTER 7). Yet, their influence on society can hardly be ignored.

In one of his novels John Grisham, the contemporary, renowned author, writes about the life of a politician-turned-lobbyist in Washington, D. C. "For years Bob Critz had watched the losers cross the street and start new careers twisting the arms of their former colleagues, selling their souls to anyone with enough money to buy whatever influence they advertised. It was such a rotten business. He was sick of the political life, but, sadly, he knew nothing else." THE BROKER, Bantam Dell, Division of Random House, New York, New York, 2005, p. 28.

The role of political parties has greatly been reduced by the introduction of television in the second half of the twentieth century. Candidates increasingly relied on TV time to portray themselves and communicate directly with the voters. But funding of the election process is so expensive that hardly a candidate can do without financial support from one of the two main political parties.

Then came social media. In 2008 the Democratic Party successfully used the Internet to get the vote out. In the 2016 presidential election, President

Donald Trump relied heavily on Twitter to get his message across to the voters. A hostile mainstream media could be circumvented by tweets.

But the fact remains that the two political parties wield a considerable degree of control over the political landscape.

Beside the financial resources at their disposal, the parties' ideology fulfills some basic human need of belonging. Many a voter selects a candidate simply because s/he belongs to the "correct" party.

In 2016 the Democratic Party lost the White House, control of the Senate, the House, and 34 governorships—33 Republican governors and one Independent. Democrats blamed everybody and everything. Protesters in big cities were shown frequently on TV. Many were not aware of why or what they were protesting.

Ron Hart, a syndicated op-ed humorist, writes,

> Lefties have one go-to reaction to anything that does not fit their narrative: protest... if George Soros... can get 10 lay-about friends together, paint some signs and alert the media, they will get inordinate TV coverage... you don't have to say what you are protesting.... As long as you are yelling about Donald Trump, you will be captured on TV. NORTH WEST FLORIDA DAILY NEWS, February 12, 2017, p. A14.

Some "protesters" are under the illusion to think that they should get free education, free health care, a nice house, and a new car. Hart goes on to say, "This is the generation our education system has raised for us, and it is in part why Trump was elected."

"Donald Trump's victory represented a rejection of Barak Obama's America," writes Patrick J. Buchanan, an author and syndicated columnist. NORTH WEST FLORIDA DAILY NEWS, January 10, 2017, p. A6.

Buchanan looks at how America has become a "liberal democratic, de-Christianized and militantly secularist," country. Our elites "welcome Third World immigration that is changing the face of America." The mainstream media celebrates the notion that all religions are equal and "should be treated equally.... America's elite... celebrate same-sex marriage and reproductive rights." *Ibid.*

France, by contrast, is moving away from liberal democracy. "At the end of the Second World War, liberal democracy—America's great export—appeared to be the future of the West if not of mankind." *Ibid.* But not anymore.

"More and more Europeans are identifying with the social values of Putin's Russia. Pro-Putin parties are surging in Europe. Pro-American parties have been facing losses and defections." *Ibid.*

How far things have changed over the past few decades!

American values used to dominate society; conservatism was the norm. Christian teachings and principles were so deeply embedded in the subconscious that no voices cried for separation of church and state. Television productions followed the unwritten rules of social decency.

But gradually and unconsciously, the dark forces of "change" got stronger and stronger.

Disguised under the banner of progressivism, societal attitudes started to drift away from what is good. Distinction between what is right and what is not got blurred. Religion was delegated to the private realm. Same-sex marriage was celebrated and even defended as a life-style. Abortion has been legalized; tax payers' money is used to fund organizations such as Planned Parenthood.

Whereas America's elite led the country deep into what is called liberalism, Europe chose to put a stop on the downward trend. "If we are the future, less and less do France and Europe appear to want that future," writes Patrick Buchanan. *Ibid.*

Although "America preaches that all religions are equal,.... France does not seem to share that liberal belief."

For many European countries, religion had for long been put on the back burner. But terrorist attacks over the past few years in France, England, Belgium, and Germany by Islamic jihadists have forced a rethinking of religious tolerance. The past few years have seen a rise in the popularity of far-right parties.

Buchanan looked at the 2017 French presidential election to prove a point. "In the final round next May [2017], the French election is likely to come down to a choice between Marine Le Pen and Francois Fillon." *Ibid.*

Although actual election results came out differently, the trend is worth exploring.

Le Pen believes in "let France be France." Fillon is a Catholic traditionalist. *Ibid.*

Le Pen wants France to "secede from the European Union and move closer to Vladimir Putin's Russia." *Ibid.* Her candidacy has been fueled by the presence of five million Muslims currently in France (about eight percent of the population), as well as the prospective arrival of millions more.

Fillon won the primary by "identifying himself as a man of Catholic beliefs and values and an opponent of same-sex marriage and abortion." He believes that "the France that was 'the eldest daughter of the church' should also be heard." *Ibid.*

Not everyone in the U.S. is happy with how the Obama administration dealt with the threat of Islamic militancy. Daniel Henninger writes,

> Future historians will have to account for the rise of the Islamic State—in Iraq, Syria, Libya, Paris, Brussels, San Bernardino, and its future bomb sites—during the years Barak Obama held office. Either there is some connection,

or it has been mere coincidence. THE WALL STREET JOURNAL, March 24, 2016, p. A15.

Henninger explains that Obama is a "transitional figure in the Democratic Party." His policies differed considerably from those of Franklin D. Roosevelt, Harry Truman, John Kennedy, Lindon Johnson, and Bill Clinton who shared a belief in "robust internationalism." *Ibid.*

Obama supporters are the "New Left progressives." They are the Democrats who "challenged their party's establishment in... Chicago in 1968, the most pivotal year in the modern history of the Democratic Party." *Ibid.*

The Cold War continued for 40 years—from shortly after the end of World War II until the collapse of the Soviet Union in 1991. The American Left dismissed the Cold War as "wasteful military spending." During that period the U.S. president was called the leader of the free world—a world united then in "containing and defeating an ideology whose publicly stated goal was to displace the liberal value of the democracies." *Ibid.*

But the end of the Cold War did not bring the long-awaited peace.

Radicalized Islam, which was started in 1928 in Egypt by Hassan El Banna who founded the Muslim Brotherhood, started to show itself on the world stage with Osama Bin Laden, who in the late 1980s was joined by Ayman El Zawahry, the Egyptian surgeon, in Afghanistan. The ideology of Islamic jihadism spread from Southeast Asia to the Middle East, North Africa, and some other African countries like Somalia, Mali, Sudan, and Nigeria. In Egypt the Muslim Brotherhood organization took control in June 2012, and Mohammed Morsi became the president of Egypt with the explicit support of the Obama administration.

Whereas the Cold War managed to unite the world, radicalized Islam split the Western world.

Europe already has millions of Islamic migrants living and working there but most remain unassimilated in society. The Islamic tide of the past two or three decades has brought terrorist acts to several European countries. Europeans, rightfully so, are getting more alarmed by the large number of refugees who are or were on their way to Europe. After the Brussels bombing, the Belgian Prime Minister said, "We are confronted with enemies who want to fight against our freedoms. We have to act to protect our way of life." *Ibid.*

The issue of radical Islam now facing the West may be coming to a solution after the end of the Obama administration.

"The now-manifest, deadly flaw in the progressive Obama foreign policy is that uncontained revolutionary ideologies today are nearly always centrifugal, overrunning national borders—Islamic State in Europe, Iran across the whole of the Middle East," writes Henninger. *Ibid.*

The political battle that has deeply divided the U.S. spilled over to engulf retailers.

After the November 2016 election, debates started over athletic shoemaker New Balance Athletics, Inc.'s support of Trump's trade policy. An anti-Trump group called Grab Your Wallet supported boycotting dozens of stores including Macy's, Inc. and L. L. Bean, Inc. On the other hand, Trump supporters are encouraging people to buy Ivanka's line of products and to boycott Starbucks Corporation for "pledging to hire 10,000 refugees."

Compromise is increasingly disappearing from the political landscape. The two main political parties used to "compromise" in order to advance the legislative process. They understood that both sides of the aisle are successful when the national interest is the ultimate goal. Not anymore. Compromise became a shameful word instead.

The unsuccessful impeachment proceedings of Bill Clinton probably signaled the beginning of a period where each party dug in its heels in support of the party. The election of the first African-American president could have worked miracles toward improving race relations but, instead, it deepened the division. The 2016 presidential election has been an epic political struggle.

In a June 2016 article, Joseph Epstein tries to answer the question, "Why Trumpkins Want Their Country Back." THE WALL STREET JOURNAL, June 11-12, 2016, p. A13.

Epstein recalls a question that was asked to Irving Kristol (who died on September 18, 2009) about the cultural wars. Kristol answered, "They are over, we lost."

By "we" he meant "people with a strong regard for tradition, who valued liberty over government-induced equality, the entrepreneurial over the entitlement spirit."

Epstein agrees with Kristol that, for the moment at least, "the struggle for tradition, liberty, and private business endeavor has been substantially stalled." *Ibid.* Instead, we have the progressivism of multiculturalism, political correctness, and victimhood as the driving social force.

One has to wonder if "multiculturalism" is to be included here as a contributing social force. The term is usually associated with immigrants from around the world. But the U.S. has *always* been a country of immigrants. Legal immigrants, in general, come to the U.S. seeking a better future for themselves and their families. They work hard—even harder than their peers—to prove themselves in their new competitive environment. About half of the Fortune 500 companies have been founded by first-generation immigrants.

The election of Donald J. Trump as the 45th president of the United States came as the response of a woman who was asked by a reporter of one of the major network news organizations why she was supporting him. The "thoroughly respectable-seeming middle-class woman" replied without hesitation, "I want my country back." *Ibid.*

What she really meant was that "she couldn't any longer bear to watch the United States on the descent, hostage to progressivist ideas that bring neither contentment nor satisfaction but instead foster a state of perpetual protest and agitation, anger and tumult." *Ibid.*

Months after the election, protest, anger, and tumult continue with no end in sight. Many a protester was asked by reporters, "What are you protesting?" There was no answer. It is widely believed that most protests are organized and financed by Democratic activists.

Politics and economics are inseparable twins; they continuously feed off of and interact with each other. So it comes as a no-brainer that the two political parties are split over their approach to the economy.

Obama's rhetoric included such slogans as "income inequality" and "attack the rich" used mainly to "sway envy-driven, simple minds," Ron Hart writes in NORTH WEST FLORIDA DAILY NEWS, January 8, 2017, p. A14. The rhetoric implied that "capitalism and entrepreneurs are bad."

"Lost on the snowflake generation is the hypocrisy of Hillary Clinton, who vowed to take on the 'excesses of capitalism' and demanded $300,000 per speech from corporations." Hart also points out actors who get $15 million per movie but call corporations "greedy."

The Democrats are bent on selling their "statist/socialist agenda." They presuppose the evils of capitalism in order to enhance their policies. But the facts are uncontested, "Free-market capitalism is a far more virtuous system of government and has done far more to improve the lot of mankind wherever it is allowed to flourish."

Consider Germany. Before its reunification, many East Germans risked and lost their lives fleeing the communist regime to go to the more prosperous and free West Germany. It was always a unidirectional process with essentially nobody going from West to East Germany.

A look at Third World countries leaves little doubt that a "strong central government and a stranglehold on business" is a failed economic policy. *Ibid.* Cuba, Venezuela, and North Korea are just some examples of widespread poverty, misery, and crime. Dictators celebrate full control as the means to stay in power.

Ron Hart goes on to say, "Capitalism did not strap us with $20 trillion—and growing—in national debt... to advance destructive dependency, political agendas, and buy votes.... Capitalism has the mechanisms to enforce good behavior—quickly." *Ibid.* When Tiger Woods' scandals became public, AT&T withdrew its support.

Whereas capitalism rewards innovation, hard work, risk-taking, honesty, and intellect, government civil service rules and regulations are mostly void of incentives and punishment. None of those involved in the "IRS scandal, Benghazigate, the Secret Service hooker scandal, or the VA mess," has paid any price. *Ibid.* During investigations before Congress, government workers take the Fifth.

It comes as no surprise that "85 percent of federal employee political donations went to Democrats." *Ibid.*

Politicians and economists share a common denominator. Each can come up with different solutions and interpretations of the same phenomenon. It has been said that if you ask the opinion of ten economists about an economic issue, you are likely to end up not with ten but 11 solutions.

In his book AVERAGE IS OVER, Tyler Cowen, an economist, suggests that "the disruptive effects of automation and ever-cheaper computer power have only just begun to be felt," writes Lexington in THE ECONOMIST, September 21, 2013, p. 35. Cowen wonders if America could "survive the end of the American Dream."

But politicians find it hard to admit to the idea. The Democrats would rather blame the Republicans for the economic woes, and vice versa.

Barack Obama called America's wealth gap "our great unfinished business." The crisis of inequality, he thinks, has been "decades in the making." Obama accused "entrenched interests of working for years to spread a 'great untruth' that government intervention is either harmful or a plot to grab tax dollars from the squeezed middle class and shower them on the undeserving poor." *Ibid.*

The Democrats claim that few Americans do very well while middle-class families struggle and fight over a shrinking economic pie.

And Republicans accuse Obama of "smothering economic opportunity with a big-government nightmare of debts [approaching $20 trillion], 'class-warfare' taxes, innovation-smothering regulation and over-generous welfare." Many are working harder and longer hours just to keep up, but "some people shun work because they can make almost as much from government benefits." *Ibid.*

The undisputed fact is that the U.S. has been built from scratch by honest, hard-working people who took pride in their work to support themselves and their families. The last few decades, however, have seen a gradual yet unmistakable shift in societal expectations and attitude. The welfare system was initially instituted to help those who could not take care of themselves due to some physical and/or mental disability.

Like with any other honorable endeavor, some people are likely to find ways to abuse the system. Teen age pregnancy was a sure way of soliciting government money. Benefits increased proportionally with the number of children. The absence of a father, or other role models, helped breed a failed generation of drug addicts and criminals. The well-intended policy had serious unintended consequences.

There are those who became experienced in finding loopholes to collect government aid by all legitimate as well as illegitimate ways. Some even feel entitled to receive such benefits as a compensation for past deeds.

Since the election of the populist Republican president in 2016, protests mushroomed in big cities. The mainstream media, who fell in love with Obama for the whole eight years, put President Trump in their cross hairs. Every criticism they could muster was lavishly poured on the new Republican administration. "Fake news" was the term used to describe news reported on CNN and MSNBC that was attributed to undisclosed sources.

Republican senators and congressmen held town hall meetings to hear their constituents back home. In February 2017 during the congressional recess, Republican legislators were met with "angry" people. Why angry? The "globalist media" keep feeding distorted notions about Donald J. Trump. Some simple-minded voters lack critical thinking skills to winnow out what is fake and what makes sense.

The 45th president is a nationalist who seeks to "Make America Great Again" by creating well-paying jobs, strengthening the military, securing our borders, and eliminating executive orders that were designed to smother economic growth. During the eight years of the Obama administration, the U.S. GDP never exceeded two percent.

Big cities embrace the majority of illegal immigrants in the U. S. "In 2014, the 20 metropolitan areas with the largest undocumented populations were home to 6.8 million, or 61 percent of the estimated 11.1 million in the country." THE WALL STREET JOURNAL, February 10, 2017, p. A2.

Greater New York and metropolitan Los Angeles are among several metropolitan areas with large undocumented populations "whose mayors have pledged not to cooperate with federal efforts to step up immigration enforcement."

Political power can trump national security not only in the U. S. but in other countries as well.

After the terrorist attack of November 2016 in Paris, the French president Francois Hollande introduced a bill that allowed authorities to withdraw French citizenship from those involved in terrorist attacks. But political gamesmanship stepped in the way. The opposition sacrificed France's national security for short-sighted political gain.

Daniel Oppenheimer's book EXIT RIGHT: THE PEOPLE WHO LEFT THE LEFT AND RESHAPED THE AMERICAN CENTURY updates the history of "political defectors." He begins with ex-Communists Whittaker Chambers and James Burnham, then talks about two renouncers of liberalism: Ronald Reagan and Norman Podhoretz, and ends with two "casualties of the '60s-'70s radical left": David Horowitz and Christopher Hitchens.

Oppenheimer writes, "The ex-believers—the heretics, the apostates—are the problem children of any politics, in any time." He laments that we expect everyone to say which side s/he is on, and forget that politics also "offers parables of second thoughts and transformation." Sam Tanenhaus, THE ATLANTIC, March 2016, pp. 42-44.

Chambers and Burnham gave up Communism as facts about the Soviet Union "had become too ugly to justify."

Reagan was a member of Hollywood's liberal left, "sometimes tangling with labor activists who didn't grasp, as he did, 'the fundamental decency, virtue, and productivity of the American people,'" Oppenheimer writes. In the 1950s Reagan was still a Democrat but studied WITNESS and NATIONAL REVIEW, whose "most august presences were Chambers and Burnham." Reagan combined their teachings with the "free-market principles he espoused" as a spokesman for General Electric.

> The result was his uniquely sunny brand of conservative homiletics, which sounded hopeful even when it included dark warnings that Medicare was the first step toward serfdom and would lead to 'other federal programs that will invade every area of freedom as we have known it in this country until one day... we will wake to find that we have Socialism.' *Ibid.*

Tanenhaus blames Chambers and Burnham for the "death-struggle atmosphere they brought to politics." He believes that modern conservatism was the "brainchild of ex-Communists who had been disillusioned by the crimes of the Soviet Revolution."

Some think of Chambers and Byrnham as "pioneers" of the "death-struggle" atmosphere that has engulfed politics. Others think that the unsuccessful impeachment of Bill Clinton during his second term in office galvanized polarization of the Left and Right.

On an optimistic note, the two-party U.S. political system offers voters a choice. Those who have experienced the stranglehold on politics by the Communist Party look with envy at those who can choose.

PART IV

PART IV: POWER OF THE INTERNET

The Creator bestowed man with a brain. Other creatures have brains too, but the human brain is unique in its ability to invent and "create" new objects.

The human brain holds ten billion cells or neurons. Some estimates put the number at 100 billion.

"No two cells are exactly the same, nor do they respond to the same incoming information in the same way." Richard A. Swenson. MORE THAN MEETS THE EYE, Navpress, Colorado Springs, Colorado, 2000 (see also CHAPTER 1).

The brain holds 10 to the 14th power bits of information, (that is, 10 with 14 zeros in front of it,) and thus "has a storage capacity one thousand times that of a Cray-2 supercomputer." *Ibid.*

Basic scientific research in the 1920s and 1930s led to the development of the computer in the early 1950s. A few decades later, research at U.S. military institutions introduced the Internet to the world. Satellite television, personal computers, and smartphones followed. And the human mind's achievements continue on.

The Internet helps in reducing fraud in the health care system and exposing false claims for welfare payments saving Americans millions if not billions of dollars.

Companies, such as LexisNexis, managed to build a trove of data using "dozens of computer racks, each holding 80 servers," linked up with each other to form a vast supercomputer. The company is helping the government "spot fraudulent requests for cash, preferably *before* the money goes out of the door." THE ECONOMIST, November 30, 2013, pp. 27-28.

In China and Vietnam the Internet provides a platform for vocal dissenters who are "often lionized through social media." THE ECONOMIST, October 26, 2013, p. 52.

The Internet helps politicians to "transmit their messages directly to voters, loosening the newspapers' grip" on national politics. THE WALL TREET JOURNAL, April 18, 2016, p. A7.

But not all the "news" is good. Negative manifestations of the Internet have been well reported.

Global Internet fraudsters are "infiltrating popular dating sites to fleece people out of their savings." THE WALL STREET JOURNAL, September, 2016, p. A3.

Internet pornography is a major concern for parents as well as society as a whole. It can distract young adults and destroy families.

In exploring the "seductive appeal" of technology, people are giving up a lot of their privacy.

The last few years have seen a heightened concern from officials and ordinary citizens about cyber security. One expert explained the danger by saying, "The Internet was not originally designed to be secure—it is more of an offensive tool." Ted Koppel. LIGHTS OUT, Crown Publishers, New York, 2015, p. 39.

All over the United States the power grid is interconnected through the Internet. This provides high efficiency since high demand in one region can be met with more supply from a lower demand part of the grid. But a well-designed, major attack can bring down the whole system causing serious, long-term damage.

CHAPTER 9

FOUNDERS AND DEVELOPERS

In the summer of 2013 Queen Elizabeth II honored five pioneers in computer networking.

Vint Cerf and Bob Khan are two American scientists who wrote the "protocols that underpin the Internet." THE ECONOMIST, November 30, 2013, pp. 19-20. Tim Berners-Lee invented the World Wide Web, Marc Andreesen created the first successful web browser, and Louis Pouzin is a Frenchman who is less well known although his "contributions to the field are every bit as seminal."

In the 1970s Pouzin introduced a new data network that "linked locations in France, Italy, and Britain." The network was simple and efficient. It attracted the attention of Dr. Cerf and Dr. Kahn who included "aspects of its design in the protocols that now power the Internet." *Ibid.*

Born in 1931 Pouzin later graduated from the Ecole Polytechnique, France's most prestigious technical institution. He then designed machine tools for the French telegraph and telecom provider.

But in the 1950s he read an article that IBM was on its way to have its computers capable of handling "all sorts of bureaucratic drudgery."

Eager to expand his career in computing, Pouzin realized that he had to learn how to program and to speak English. He got a two-year sabbatical at the Massachusetts Institute of Technology (MIT) that gave him the chance to do both.

In the early 1960s Pouzin moved his family to the United States. He got involved in "pioneering teamwork on time-sharing systems" that aimed to enable several users to run programs simultaneously thus making better use of the expensive mainframe computers. Pouzin created a program that helped users "automate tedious and repetitive commands." *Ibid.*

In 1971 France launched an ambitious plan to "bolster the country's computing industry." Pouzin was asked to lead research on a national computer network.

He visited U.S. universities to learn about ARPANET, a "network that had been switched on two years before." But Pouzin regarded ARPANET as inefficient. Every computer required a "complex piece of hardware to link it to the network.... Packets of information traveled in strict order from one station to another." *Ibid.*

Pouzin's team came up with a simpler way to achieve networking. CYCLADES depends on a "connectionless packet-switching [which] reduced the need for... costly equipment within the network to establish predetermined routs for packets." *Ibid.* This also made it easier to link up different networks. In 1973 CYCLADES was used to connect networks between Paris and Grenoble.

Dr. Cerf and Dr. Khan built upon Pouzin's connectionless, "datagram-based approach, so that concepts from CYCLADES found their way into the TCP/IP suite of protocols on which the modern Internet now runs." *Ibid.*

Pouzin supports researchers in America, Ireland, and Spain who are devising ways to make the Internet more efficient and secure. He says that the Internet was created "as an experimental network.... It still is one.... A century from now it must not be the same." *Ibid.*

The Internet has been an instrumental tool in extending the horizon of available information made easier by developments in the hardware. Mainframe computers developed into personal computers, laptops, tablets, iPads, and smartphones. All are dependent on the Internet which remains largely insecure. Hacking and identity theft are increasingly becoming a daily threat for some (CHAPTER 10).

Yet the technological revolution has its footprint on almost all aspects of modern life. With the widespread use of gadgets, a new class of tech elite has emerged. "The tech elite will join bankers and oilmen in public demonology," predicts Adrian Wooldridge. THE ECONOMIST, The World in 2014, p. 34.

Wooldridge describes Sean Parker's multimillion dollar wedding. The 364 guests were dressed in Tolkein-inspired costumes "designed by the woman who created the costumes for 'The LORD OF THE RINGS.'" Parker founded Napster and was Facebook's first president.

Mark Zuckerberg owns 29.3 percent of Facebook; Larry Ellison owns 24 percent of Oracle. This contrasts with investment in oil where the largest single investor in Exxon Mobil controls just 0.04 percent of the stocks.

"The Silicon elite will cease to be regarded as geeks who happen to be filthy rich and become filthy rich people who happen to be geeks," writes Wooldridge.

The tech elite turned out to be some of the most "ruthless capitalists around." *Ibid.*

A handful of oligopolies dominates the tech economy. Google and Apple provide more than 90 percent of the operating systems for smartphones. "Facebook has more than half of North Americans and Europeans as its customers." *Ibid.*

Google has a market cap of $290 billion. This makes the tech company "six times bigger than GM but employs only around a fifth as many workers." *Ibid.*

Silicon Valley is not only generating billionaires and millionaires but also thousands of young graduates who pull in more than $100,000 a year.

Amassing wealth helps techies upping their profile in politics. They employ a large number of Washington lobbyists. Some even started to buy media outlets. Jeff Bezos bought THE WASHINGTON POST, and Chris Hughes bought THE NEW REPUBLIC.

Social media has been consuming the attention of society: young and old, rich and poor, educated and illiterate. The vanity of man and his endless appetite for fame and popularity propelled social networks to prime status. MySpace, Facebook, Snapchat, WhatsApp, and Instagram are platforms that allow users to share photos and information—mostly about themselves. "With 1.2 billion users, Facebook is the dominant force." THE ECONOMIST, January 4, 2014, pp. 49-50.

As the keynote speaker at the 2016 annual Facebook conference for developers, Mark Zuckerberg said, "We are one global community... with the aspiration to give everyone the power to share everything with anyone." L. Gordon Crovitz, THE WALL STREET JOURNAL, April 18, 2016, p. A13.

Would Zuckerberg's vision materialize?

"China has invoked 'Internet sovereignty' to build its own set of networks cut off from the rest of the world."

Authoritarian regimes in Russia, Iran, Turkey, and others routinely ban sites including Facebook.

Scott Malcomson, communications consultant, describes the "Internet's fall from its founding aspirations" in his book SPLINTERNET: HOW GEOPOLITICS AND COMMERCE ARE FRAGMENTING THE WORLD WIDE WEB.

> In the early years, the Internet and geek culture split off from government, launching a period of spectacular innovation, excitement, and profit.

Malcomson cites John Perry Barlow's 1996 declaration, "Governments of the industrial world... I ask you of the past to leave us alone.... You have no sovereignty where we gather."

The communications consultant acknowledges that the Internet was "bound to become less free as it matured," but he puts much of the blame on policy changes in Washington.

Over the past few years the Obama administration has "abandoned the American exceptionalism that built the Internet as we know it." The 44th president decided in 2014 that he would end "U.S. stewardship over the global Internet." The U.S. has a contract with the Internet Corporation for Assigned Names and Numbers (ICANN) that allows ICANN to protect the root zone of web names and addresses. The contract empowered U.S. developers and engineers to "build networks free of pressure from other governments." *Ibid.*

By surrendering U.S. control over the Internet, the last president vied to make it possible for authoritarian regimes to censor the Internet globally and not just in their own countries.

> Mr. Obama once famously declared that government, not entrepreneurs, had built the Internet. That wasn't true, but... If Washington continues to abandon its commitment to the open Internet, the dreams of digital innovators around the world will be crushed. *Ibid.*

A question then springs to mind Who would benefit from such policies? Freedom-loving people? Some tend to think of it as part of the New World Order where the United States (the father of the Internet) surrenders its protection of the World Wide Web.

CHAPTER 10

A POSITIVE TOOL

Online college education, cutting fraud in national healthcare expenditures, online merchandising, and even connecting clients to non-professional drivers are but some examples of how the Internet has proliferated in our daily life making it easier, faster, and less expensive.

With budgets in the red, state contributions to institutions of higher education have been dwindling over the past several years. Higher tuition is forcing students into amassing debt. Default on student loans has reached alarming proportions.

Some hope that the Internet will "revolutionize higher education, making it cheaper and more accessible to the masses." On the other hand, some academics "worry that they will be sacked and replaced by videos of their... colleagues." THE ECONOMIST, October 12, 2013, p. 41.

In 2011 online education courses reached 6.7 million students. "A third of those enrolled at traditional colleges took an online course as part of their degrees."

With a budget deficit of $439 billion in fiscal year 2015 and a debt of 74 percent of the GDP, "the federal government embraced the work done by LexisNexis—an online-information firm that is part of Reed Elsevier. THE ECONOMIST, November 30, 2013, pp. 27-28.

"Losses from healthcare scams alone are between $70 billion and $240 billion a year," reckons the FBI. Even higher percentages of frauds are being committed through stolen identities. False claims for welfare payments, and false tax refunds are some examples. Rashia Wilson, self-described as the first lady of tax-refund fraud, claimed "bogus rebates of more than $11 million." *Ibid.*

In 2012 about 12.6 million people were victimized by identity theft in the United States.

LexisNexis, located in north Atlanta, has "dozens of computer racks, each holding 80 servers, linked up with each other and with a sister site in Boca Raton to form a vast supercomputer." *Ibid.* The database held by these black boxes amounts to five petabytes (PB), that is 10 to the power 15 bytes, or 10 with 15 zeros beside it, or one million gigabytes (GB).

The trove of data includes property, vehicle registration as well as other "public records, legal findings, and proprietary data bought from firms that serve computers." *Ibid.*

LexisNexis is also cooperating with other information providers including credit bureaus, such as Equifax and Experian to develop its "risk solutions" business. This, in part, is helping the federal government "spot fraudulent requests for cash, preferably before the money goes out of the door." *Ibid.*

About 30 state and federal agencies are using "filters" designed by LexisNexis to flag suspicious requests. Applications for cash are run against the millions of names, addresses, and other personal information in the company database. If the same address appears on a number of cash requests, fraud is quickly identified. This would have taken months to spot by manual investigation.

Not surprisingly, the Georgia Department of Revenue was a pioneer. In 2012, four million tax returns were filed. Of those, 160,000 were found to be suspicious. The total savings amounted to $110 million. The Georgia revenue commissioner attributes $23 million of that amount directly to the fraud filters which "cost just $3 million to set up and run."

Of the 50 states, Florida has the highest rate of identity theft. Miami and Tampa are at the top of the list of the five major U.S. cities with the highest fraudulent tax returns. (The other three are Atlanta, Detroit, and Houston.)

Florida is more susceptible to such scams due to its crowds of pensioners and the large number of non-English-speaking immigrants who can be "easily duped into disclosing personal information." *Ibid.* Another contributing factor is Florida's high number of people who do not have enough income to require filing tax returns. This means many stolen numbers can avoid detection because they do not generate duplicate filings.

In 2011 Tampa police found that many people stopped by authorities have "lists of stolen IDs on them." *Ibid.*

The Florida Department of Children and Families started a four-county pilot project with LexisNexis. The department doles out Medicaid payments, food stamps, and cash assistance. The filters flagged "dodgy online applications at an annualized rate of $60 million," which is more than 50 times the project's cost. It was decided to extend the project to the whole state of Florida. A woman who was claiming food stamps in all 50 states was caught.

Based in San Francisco, Uber connects clients to non-professional drivers through its low-cost UberPop service. In Paris, French taxi drivers were infuriated and prompted charges against the company. "Uber risks millions of euros in damages and fines." NORTH WEST FLORIDA DAILY NEWS, February 26, 2016, p. A10. Two of the company's top executives were accused of complicity in protecting an illegal taxi activity.

Traditional French taxi drivers, represented by dozens of taxi unions and associations, complained that Uber sidesteps taxes, social charges, and licensing fees.

In 2014 the French Parliament voted to outlaw UberPop (and other similar services). Uber suspended its UberPop service in France in July 2015.

But this was not enough. Uber's standard app-based service still causes occasional strikes and clashes with taxi drivers.

Apart from legalities and the sensitive issue of nationalism, the fact remains that the Internet is changing our way of life, making it easier, faster, and less expensive. The impact is world wide.

And new innovations continue. The U.S. has been leading the way since the birth of the Internet in the 1970s.

But the most crucial impact of the Internet is in the area of human rights and freedom.

By definition, autocratic regimes imply a ruler with absolute power. To maintain control over the populace the system keeps a tight reign on the media. Dissent has no means of expressing itself. The Internet has opened a door for the oppressed.

> In China,... those who stand up are often lionized through social media. In Vietnam,... a crackdown has taken place this year on vocal online dissent, with dozens locked up and new limits on online discourse. THE ECONOMIST, October 26, 2013, p. 52.

In an attempt to reclaim the monopoly on all sources of mass media, the Vietnamese Communist Party has enacted laws to only allow the exchange of personal information online. Exchange of news articles are forbidden. However, the attempt seems to be doomed. "Even if the crackdown were enforceable,... the cynicism... is smoldering in Vietnam, as in China." *Ibid.*

In both countries, government control of the Internet is fueling the perception that party leaders are more interested in "protecting their own power" than in the national good.

In Sofia, Bulgaria thousands of Bulgarians have taken to the streets for almost 100 days in 2013. Some protests have occurred in other big Bulgarian cities. The protesters represent "all strata" of society though the "majority seem to be young, educated, and middle class." THE ECONOMIST, September 21, 2013, p. 56. The demonstrators have their own websites, Facebook page, and a Twitter hashtag.

In Turkey the Islamist president Recep Tayyip Erdogan got 51.2 percent of the vote on a set of new laws that gave him more powers. The referendum was considered one of the "most important votes" since the republic's founding in 1923. The Organization for Security and Cooperation in Europe (OSCE) reported its concern about the "integrity of Turkey's justice system following a failed coup attempt in July 2016." THE WALL STREET JOURNAL, April 18, 2017, pp. A1, A7.

Three of the 11 members of the high electoral board and the chairs of 221 lower boards were "purged and replaced since July 2016." About one third of all judges have been "dismissed or detained" during the same period. Military officers and journalists did not fare better.

CHAPTER 11

UNINTENDED CONSEQUENCES

Man has the uncanny tendency to convert the positive into a liability. Created to enjoy paradise, Adam chose to rebel against the Creator. Sin led to his expulsion from God's favor. But God's mercy on mankind has been manifested in sending His only begotten Son. He took the form of a mortal and preached God's love and forgiveness before His crucifixion and ascension into heaven. Until Christ's second coming, man has the choice between good and evil.

On April 21, 2017 THE NORTHWEST FLORIDA DAILY NEWS had an article titled "Increasingly social media is anti-social." The article listed a number of disturbing incidents that took place in the span of less than four months from January to April 2017. All have been streamed live on Facebook.

Early in January four black people in Chicago kidnapped an 18-year-old mentally ill white man, beat, and tortured him in an "anti-Trump fit."

Later in the same month a 14-year-old from Miami streamed her own suicide by hanging after she had been in and out of foster care.

In March back in Chicago a gang of "teen-aged thugs" kidnapped and raped a 15-year-old girl while at least 40 people watched but reported nothing.

On April 16 a 74-year-old man was approached by Steve W. Stephens who asked him to repeat a woman's name and then "shot him in cold blood" after he did so. Stephens recorded the incident and posted it on Facebook.

Has the tool that, in one respect, was supposed to inform, entertain, and perhaps unite us by expanding the reach of virtual community failed to maintain boundaries of decency, law-abiding behavior, and respect for human dignity? *Ibid.*

One may contrast the above cases with not so long ago when the print news media abstained from reporting suicides, except in rare cases, so as not to "shock or tantalize" or induce copycats. But with the advent of social media, those days are gone forever.

The urge to be immediately famous, or rather infamous, on social media through criminal behavior seems a "potent draw," until the "better angels... overcome the wickedness residing in the hearts of some," as Abraham Lincoln said in his first inaugural address. *Ibid.*

Not all misgivings are as grim as the ones reported above.

"Online Daters Are Falling Prey to Scams," is the title of an article in THE WALL STREET JOURNAL, September 1, 2016, p. A3. The Internet provided a platform for singles to meet. A legitimate goal, however, is bringing a lot of heartache to some good, trusting people.

Fraudsters are using dating sites to "fleece people out of their savings." Swindlers lift photos of real people from the Internet and use them to create profiles.

Scammers usually claim to be Americans working temporarily overseas. The "relationship" starts with a grooming process in which the suitor plays on the feelings of the future victim. Then he starts talking about some emergency that requires him to have money as a "loan," since his own funds are presently tied up. Requests for loans continue with new excuses.

"Victims lost nearly $120 million to 'romance scams' in the first six months of 2016." *Ibid.*

A different type of scammers is emerging in Canada. They may better be called 'freeloaders' who "try to avoid financial obligations by claiming to be Freemen, Detaxers, followers of Moorish Law, members of the Church of the Ecumenical Redemption International, or of other assorted groups." THE ECONOMIST, October 12, 2013, p. 46.

Some estimates believe that 30,000 Canadians share the belief that the government has no authority over them and can not even arrest them.

Stephen Kent of the University of Alberta believes the increase in the number of "obstructionists" is partly a spillover from the United States and partly the result of the global financial crisis and the disorientation it caused.

The Internet has made it possible for "gurus to spread their views and sell DVDs, often to badly educated and unemployed young men in rural areas." *Ibid.*

Similar movements have been reported in countries like Britain, Ireland, Australia, and New Zealand.

The ease and convenience of shopping online come at a price: privacy. THE ECONOMIST states that "abolishing privacy is the next big trend in American shopping," January 4, 2014, p. 22. Merchants dream of being able to rummage through a customer's online searches to learn about his or her shopping interests so they can send sales pitches that flash up on the customer's phone.

The invasion of privacy has been the source of widespread public outcry. This might explain the muted public response to Edward Snowden's leaks about "American cyber-spying." The biggest uproar was generated abroad. Brazil's president, at the time, called off a visit to the United States. Politicians and the press in Germany were more outraged about reports that the National Security Agency (NSA) agents targeted Chancellor

Angela Merkel. The European Parliament is "keener on debating the NSA than Congress is in Washington." *Ibid.*

During the 2016 presidential elections, the Republican front-runner Donald Trump used Twitter to "engage the public more aggressively than his rivals." THE WALL STREET JOURNAL, April 18, 2016, p. A7. He had 7.6 million followers, Hillary Clinton had 5.93 million, and Bernie Sanders had an audience of 1.97 million.

But the downside for then-candidate Donald Trump's "unrestrained" approach landed him in trouble. It turned out that he shared "messages from accounts that appear to be tied to white supremacists." *Ibid.*

The aggressive use of Twitter also makes the user more vulnerable to engaging with a category of accounts called "fake" accounts. They are called this because they "appear automated to some degree and aren't associated with a real person." *Ibid.* Some of these accounts promote extremist or offensive views.

Still candidate Donald Trump became the Republican Party nominee and then the 45th president of the United States, thanks to a well-run election campaign, a popular message, and hard work.

George Will eloquently addressed the negative impact of the Internet in an article titled: "Our National Scrouge of Misinformation." NORTH WEST FLORIDA DAILY NEWS, April 9, 2017, p. 10A.

Will refers to Tom Nichols' new book, THE DEATH OF EXPERTISE: THE CAMPAIGN AGAINST ESTABLISHED KNOWLEDGE AND WHY IT MATTERS. Nichols says that our gadgets and social media are producing people who confuse "Internet gazing" with real research, and this faux research (on the Internet) with higher education. In those years between high school and the first real job, students "demand to run institutions that the students insist should treat them as fragile children."

Today's therapeutic culture seems to be designed "to validate every opinion and feeling" regardless of whether it makes sense or not. The consequence is that there will rarely be "disagreement without anger between thin-skinned people who can not distinguish the phrase 'you are wrong' from 'you are stupid.'" *Ibid.*

To equate "critical thinking" with "relentless criticism" leads to the indiscriminate rejection of real experts. In their place we have a "google-fueled, Wikipedia-based, blog-sodden" disdain for even the ideal of expertise.

A family doctor tells about patients in their twenties who argue with their physician about what they read on the Internet and insist on sticking with their Internet-posted information.

The Internet with all of its merits has been helping in "spreading epidemic misinformation," now known as "alternative facts." Needless to say it is *man,* not the Internet, who carries all the blame.

A smartphone provides more information "than ever existed in the entire Library of Alexandria," Nichols says. This is likely to produce a "self-deluding veneer of erudition."

The present state of affairs has been in development for some time.

George Will in his article refers to Lynne Truss, who in 2005 published her book TALK TO THE HAND: THE UTTER BLOODY RUDENESS OF THE WORLD TODAY. She said that we were slouching into "an age of social autism" with a "Universal Eff-off Reflex."

Long before streaming brought us binge watching, she foresaw people "entertaining themselves into inanition with portable technologies that enable limitless self-absorption." Truss predicted the coming of an age of "hair-trigger sensitivity" and "lazy moral relativism combined with aggressive social insolence."

Twelve years after Truss's book, a Wellesley College professor said in March 2017 that inviting "controversial, aka conservative, speakers to campus injures students by forcing them to 'invest time and energy in rebutting the speakers' arguments.'"

Lately Carolyn Stewart of the Hudson Institute writes in <u>THE AMERICAN INTEREST</u> that people "have taken an expectation that previously applied to the private sphere—control over our environment—and are increasingly applying it to the public sphere."

Stewart points out that social media's "self-affirming feedback loop" encourages "expectations for a custom-made reality" and an anger about anything "that deviates from our preferences."

The lines between the private and the public spheres have been blurred, made possible by social media. A tool of entertainment has morphed into a social ill.

CHAPTER 12

THE VULNERABLE
POWER GRID

Over the short span of two decades, the Internet has come to dominate almost all aspects of our modern daily life. Its efficiency is, however, counterbalanced by the risk of a cyber attack. "The Internet itself was not designed to keep anybody out. It was created to be universally accessible." Ted Koppel, LIGHTS OUT, Crown Publishers, New York, 2015, p. 39.

A noble goal is becoming increasingly susceptible to *man's* aggression and insidious attitude.

The electric power grid is "surpassingly vulnerable to cyber attack." Ted Koppel explained how and why the power grid reached such a state of vulnerability.

In August 2003, a high-voltage power line brushed against some trees and shut down. The same day three other power lines failed, "forcing the surrounding grid to take on additional current." Within a couple of hours these overburned lines fell resulting in the "largest blackout in North American history." *Ibid.* For up to two days, 50 million people lost power in an area extending from Southeastern Canada to eight northeastern states.

A U. S.-Canadian task force was formed. It concluded that the grid was vulnerable to a malicious cyber attack and warned that "hackers could inflict even greater and longer-lasting damage." *Ibid.*

The scope of the power outage of 2003 left no choice for the industry but to reluctantly take "modest steps toward accepting mandatory cyber security standards." *Ibid.*

The majority of electric power companies are privately owned. This has been the case for quite some time when relatively few companies owned the plants that generated electricity. They also owned the "transmission facilities and the equipment that ultimately delivered power to schools, businesses, hospitals, and homes." *Ibid.* Because these few companies were heavily invested in the power grid, the managers were attentive to every aspect of the electric system.

Slowly, in one state after another "that system has given way to one characterized by limited competition." *Ibid.* Now, one company in some location generates power that is transmitted by a separately-managed network and eventually delivered to the consumer by yet another company.

The fragmentation of the industry had some unintended consequences.

"Because the system's maintenance and protection reside in so many different hands and... its complexity has made each player more dependent on computerized control systems," the power grid became more vulnerable than before. The prevalence of interconnections created new pathways through which hackers could initiate a cyber attack.

Industry leaders have invested heavily in resources to protect their infrastructure. But the smaller companies have difficulty adjusting their limited budgets to spend a great deal on cyber security. Companies with "lean profit margins" became weak points in the shared responsibility of protecting the grid. As with any other chain, the electric power grid is only as strong as its weakest link.

> Breaking up the industry into a marketplace of
> interconnected parts introduced competition, which
> lowered prices. It also increased the system's vulnerability
> to cyber intrusion. *Ibid*, p. 35.

The electric power grid covers thousands of miles across different geographic areas. To maximize efficiency, overall "balance between demand and supply" has to be coordinated.

In winter Chicago needs more electricity between 2:00 and 5:00 P.M. Florida Gulf Power has more capacity than it needs in the winter. To transfer power from Florida to Chicago, high-tension power lines are needed, but communities are "inclined to object to the presence of high-tension wires" near their homes.

To coordinate, the industry has set up "regional transmission organizations and independent system operators" to monitor the amount of electricity transmitted and ensure that transmission lines do not become overburdened.

"This monitoring process... creates a dangerous point of vulnerability.... If someone were able to hack into an RTO or ISO [monitoring device] and deliberately overload the lines," the impact would be detrimental to the power grid. *Ibid*. A hacker can produce "cascading, potentially catastrophic outages."

It is fair to say that deregulation of the power industry has created a system with "more vulnerable points of entry than ever existed previously."

Before the proliferation of the Internet, the major power stations were operated by manual controls. In a few cases when one company owned a computer, it was unique to that company. But nowadays, within any one of the three U.S. grids "almost all operational phases of thousands of power companies are interconnected." *Ibid*.

There is no doubt that the system is thus highly efficient, "eliminating waste while establishing a precise balance" between demand and supply. We have chosen efficiency over resiliency.

The choice is fabulous provided that we live in a peaceful, perfect world. *But do we? Why not?*

Koppel writes on page 223, "The Internet as a weapons system has traditional applications for governments seeking to project power, but its accessibility is not exclusive to nation-states." *Individuals*, alone or as part of small groups, have become so technologically sophisticated to the point that they can "undermine the critical infrastructure of a state."

In 2010 a United States congressman got worried about vulnerability of the power grid.

Ed Markey solicited the opinions of some of the top national security experts. "Almost every national security expert warned" of the risk associated with the electric grid, but officials at the Department of Homeland Security "insist that the grid is resilient." *Ibid*.

A few years after Ed Markey's attempt to raise the national concern about the vulnerability of the power grid, George Cotter produced his fourth white paper in a series titled <u>SECURITY IN THE NORTH AMERICAN GRID—A NATION AT RISK</u>, April 2015. As the former chief scientist at the National Security Agency (NSA), Cotter sends his white papers to policy makers and federal institutions charged with homeland defense.

In his white paper George Cotter writes,

> With adversaries' malware in the National Grid, the nation has little or no chance of withstanding a major cyber attack on the North American electrical system. Incredibly weak cyber security standards... guarantees success to major nation-states and competent hackivists. This [electric power] industry is simply unrealistic in believing in the resiliency of this Grid subject to a sophisticated attack.

In October 2012 Leon Panetta, then secretary of defense, exposed serious concerns about a cyber attack. Talking to security executives Panetta warned that a rogue nation or extremist group could launch "a destructive cyber-terrorist attack [that] could virtually paralyze the nation." *Ibid*. Potential threats cited by the secretary of defense at the time included deliberate derailing of trains, contamination of urban water supplies, and shutdown of the power grid across large parts of the country.

What makes a cyber attack even more worrisome is the inability of the attacked to identify precisely the source of the attack. A counterstrike may thus be directed at the wrong target.

"Neither the American public nor the international community has come to terms yet with the notion that a major cyber attack would mount to an act of war." *Ibid*.

A cyber-terrorist attack could essentially cripple the country's economy for a rather long period of time without costing the aggressor a dime. This would be a war that is different from any previous war the world has ever known.

Consider a country like Iran. With a defense budget of $30 billion, Iran is no match for the U. S. with a defense budget of about $600 billion in 2015. But Iran can pursue its strategic goal of defeating the "Great Satan" by other means, such as terrorism and cyber warfare.

In February 2015 Ashton Carter, then secretary of defense, released a 33-page cyber security strategy.

Ted Koppel described the document as an "interesting exercise in deliberate ambiguity, in that cyber intrusions—espionage, theft, distributed denial-of-service attacks against U. S. interests—are a daily occurrence." Whereas the strategy provides a bold warning, the question of "what constitutes a red line is left deliberately unclear."

A few months after the inauguration of Donald J. Trump as the 45th president of the United States, the White House issued an executive order that declared cyber security a federal government concern. The May 11, 2017 executive order assigned each secretary the responsibility for cyber security in his/her department but would keep the federal government informed of the progress.

Over the May 13-14, 2017 weekend, 150 nations were hacked by a cyber attack.

Thomas Grove of <u>THE WALL STREET JOURNAL</u> reported about a rehearsal for cyber warfare in an "exercise that tested the North Atlantic Treaty Organization's readiness to repel hackers." May 1st, 2017, p. A9.

Late in April 2017 nearly 900 cyber security experts from Europe and the United States gathered in Tallinn, Estonia to participate in an event that focused on "defending a fictional country against a simulated cyber attack." *Ibid.* The event marked the 10-year anniversary of cyber attacks that crippled Estonia's digital infrastructure.

CHAPTER 13

SPITITUAL IMPACT

Like many other tools, the Internet has found its positive applications but nevertheless some negative ones have also popped up. The last two chapters discussed some of the Internet's man-made problems.

But there is a certain area where the Internet has opened a wide door for many to see the *light*.

"Before... printing, the Scribes wrote the Old Testament by hand. Printing the Bible contributed significantly to the spread of Christianity. Centuries later, the Internet is, and has been, a formidable tool in helping the spread of the Christian faith." Safwat Bishara, <u>TWO DIFFERENT RELIGIONS. HOW ISLAM PERCEIVES CHRISTIANITY AND WHAT IS THE TRUTH</u>, Authorhouse, Bloomington, Indiana, 2013, p. 123.

Not surprisingly, the culture of Muslim-majority countries stands in great contrast to Western culture with its deep roots in Christianity.

In Muslim nations Islam is the framework that encompasses *all* aspects of life. Social behavior and norms are dictated by Islamic teachings.

Muslim clerics and imams "oppose questioning, arguments, and discussion" by students of the faith. The phenomenon has been reported by many "open-minded Muslims" who had the audacity to question some of the Islamic teachings, bringing on themselves punishment and ostracism. *Ibid.*

"The ostentatious practices of Muslims allow for close societal judgment" of other followers of the faith. Family, friends, and neighbors pay attention to whether you "go to pray at the mosque, and if a woman covers her hair and uses the veil." *Ibid.*

Peer pressure in Islamic societies is as intense as it can be.

For centuries the clerics and imams have had complete monopoly on the preaching, teaching, and interpreting of Islam. This fits especially well in societies with high rates of illiteracy. Interestingly, the imams and clerics themselves are not educated. There are no requirements for anyone to be an imam. It is just enough to memorize a few verses from the Qur'an.

"Muslims raised in Muslim-dominated societies never before had the opportunity to privately hear and know the teachings of Christianity." *Ibid.* It is taboo to listen to a sermon delivered by a pastor or a priest or to read the Bible.

But the Internet had "opened a window on the outside world." A Muslim nowadays can "communicate, read, and see how the West—essentially Christian—is prospering. Some even have the choice to listen to, or watch, sermons broadcast by satellites." *Ibid.*

It is increasingly becoming common knowledge, at least with Christians in the Middle East, that many Muslims are converting to Christianity. The Church can not dwell on the subject for obvious reasons. The converts, too, keep a low profile or leave their country. The punishment for a Muslim who abandons Islam is ostracism at best and murder at worst.

In his book titled THE TWELFTH IMAM, Tyndale House Publishers, Carol Stream, Illinois, 2011, p. 316, Joel C. Rosenberg writes,

> ... the increasing access to the Internet and Satellite TV seemed to exacerbate people's despair. Why? Because now, for the first time in 14 centuries,... [they] could see and hear and practically taste the intellectual, economic, and

spiritual freedom and opportunity that people elsewhere in the world were experiencing. Starved... [they] were desperately seeking such freedom and opportunity for themselves.

Social media and instant communication, both brain children of the Internet, have empowered people who for long were deprived exposure to the outside world. The Internet has broken the monopoly of clerics and imams on Islam.

PART V

PART V: POWER OF AUTHORITY

Authority comes with the territory. A first-level supervisor has authority over his underlings. The CEO of a Fortune 500 company has authority over thousands of employees.

Power, on the other hand, is subtle. The son-in-law of the CEO has *power* regardless of his own rank or position in the organization. Over dinner he communicates informally with the occupant of the corner office, the status symbol. The son-in-law has no *authority* over anyone, yet he has *power*.

But power and authority are not mutually exclusive. Those who have authority wield power too.

In many countries the husband has absolute authority over his wife. Countries in Latin America and the Middle East are known examples.

Part V describes how those who have authority exercise their power over others, whether they are individuals, groups of people, or even nations.

CHAPTER 14

OVER WOMEN

The September 21, 2013, issue of <u>THE ECONOMIST</u> has an article about "Violence against Women in Latin America," on p. 39.

> Unpunished violent crime is a more general problem in the region. Nevertheless, the statistics of violence against women are particularly gruesome.... UN Women, a UN agency, found that many Latin American countries have a higher-than-average incidence of domestic violence... a woman is assaulted every 15 seconds in San Paulo, Brazil's largest city.

Between 2011 and 2012 Colombia saw a four-fold increase in attacks in which acid is thrown in women's faces. A UN report that ranked 25 countries in the world with "high" or "very high" incidences of femicides found that more than half are in the Americas, with El Salvador "the worst in the world." *Ibid.*

Many attribute the phenomenon to the fact that most cases of violence against women are not investigated, "let alone effectively prosecuted." From January to March 2013, 1,822 rapes were reported in the Brazilian state of Rio de Janeiro but only 70 men were arrested.

"Machismo has deep cultural roots in the region" and will need decades to change. But in the meantime women expect their governments to vigorously apply the existing laws to prevent and punish the aggressors.

In 1994 Latin American countries signed what is called the Convention of Belem. It requires these countries to "educate their people about women's rights, to fight machismo, and to pass laws to protect women from violence." *Ibid.* Most have done so. But the trouble is that in many cases these new laws made little difference.

Unlike in Latin America, women in the Middle East suffer not from violence as much as from social restrictions that sometimes amount to ostracism. Saudi Arabia provides an example of how women rank in Islamic societies.

A Saudi woman until very recently can not drive a car by herself. A male has to be in her company. When she leaves home to run an errand, a male has to be with her.

The Islamic faith allows a man to marry up to four women at a time. The husband can divorce the wife at "the drop of a hat" and has as many concubines as he can afford with no maximum limit.

The Saudi prince, much younger than the typical Saudi monarchs, is said to have a more Western view of women's status. Time will tell whether he will be able to placate the powerful, deeply rooted religious forces that have always favored the status quo.

In an attempt to reform women's status in the kingdom, a program initiated by the British council and run by academics from Durham Business School aims to teach Saudi women leadership capabilities.

"Managing under the Abaya," is the title of an article in the September 21, 2013 issue of THE ECONOMIST. In Saudi Arabia few women hold positions of power, and "there are few industries in which they are allowed to pursue careers," p. 70.

Inherit in the Saudi social structure is that a woman can rarely be a man's boss. "Women can not make and implement decisions themselves... [so] they must learn to influence men without seeming to direct them." The program aims to build women's confidence and help them form networks that enable them to exert more influence as a group.

Assertive body language is an essential leadership skill. But women wear an abaya, a full-length cloak, while others use a niqab which covers the face completely. Communication gets harder when the eyes, the windows of the soul, are hidden. To compensate for this shortcoming, women learn to use voice control.

An American law firm hired the first female Saudi lawyer early in 2013. The company had to build her a "separate office, to ensure that she could not mix with her male colleagues." *Ibid*. Old habits die hard.

Another form of destructive use of authority is the practice of "aborting female fetuses." Instead of attacking grown-up women (as in some Latin American countries) or willfully ignoring their human rights (as in Saudi Arabia), China and other Asian countries murder females early on—in the womb.

As the most populous (1.371 billion in 2015) nation in the world, China used birth control to limit population growth. A family could have only one child; others must be aborted. This led some families to abort the fetus if it were a female, on the hopes that the second one would be a boy.

Gradually, however, the policy has been relaxed allowing for two or three children per family. Nature has more room to take its course.

But "son-preference, once suppressed, is reviving alarmingly," in China as well as in the Caucasus. THE ECONOMIST, September 21, 2013, p. 54.

Boys are more vulnerable to childhood diseases. To compensate, nature "allows" that "105 boys are born for every 100 girls." *Ibid*. The slight preponderance of boys at birth favors equal numbers of both sexes at adulthood.

But when *man* interferes with the Creator's equilibrium, distortions occur. Aborting female fetuses disturbs the optimum 1:1 ration needed for building families and social stability.

"In Armenia and Azerbaijan more than 115 boys are born for every 100 girls, and in Georgia the ratio is 120." The three countries have seen a sharp increase in the number of boys since 1991. "The gap is second only to China's." *Ibid.*

An ultrasound machine can detect the sex of a fetus. Before the collapse of the Soviet Union in December 1991, ultrasound equipment was rare because "parts had military use and their export from the West was banned." *Ibid.* After the demise of the Eastern Bloc, the machines spread and with that sex-selective abortions increased.

Interference with nature's course is not restricted to murdering female fetuses.

Decades ago the farmers in a small village in a North African nation noticed an alarming increase in the number of stray cats. Leaders organized a full-fledged campaign to eradicate the cats. And they did. But gradually the rats took over.

The misguided approach to solving a problem is likely to create a different kind of problem.

The Creator has set in motion an order for the animal kingdom on the ground, the birds of the air, and living creatures in the water. A given species feeds on a second species, which in turn feeds on a third species, and so on. The Divine power provides that no species vanish and no species dominate over the others.

CHAPTER 15

OVER HUMANITY

It may not be practically possible to list all incidents of the abuse of power all over the world but a sample would suffice.

From Africa to Asia and from North to Central to South America, cases abound. Some are more brutal than others, but in all a person or a group of people representing a political party or an organization step over the line into the territory of inhumanity.

"The Communist Party branch secretary of the biology department at Peking University was immediately singled out as a capitalist roader" at the start of the Chinese cultural revolution. THE ATLANTIC, April 2016, p. 15. He describes how a guard, a biology student, had devised this punishment: "Open your eyes wide, look straight at the sun, and don't blink or you'll get a beating."

All through history from primitive feudal societies built on slavery to modern democratic societies, has anyone devised such a punishment?

The Central African Republic has been embroiled in civil war for quite some time. The brutality of the conflict led the United Nations to send troops to the African country.

On March 31, 2016 FRANCE 24 NEWS OUTLET announced that there were 108 victims of child abuse by none other than UN peacekeepers.

Those who are supposed to *protect* people became abusers of power. French authorities did not condemn any French soldier since 2014.

A year later, on June 20, 2017, FRANCE 24.COM reported that the UN is sending 600 troops from the Republic of Congo back home because of sex abuse claims and other misconduct in the Central African Republic. Guinea, also in Africa, suffers from a different type of power abuse.

In September 2013 the country had its first general election since 2002. But "accusations of fraud have been flying... and mistrust is rife." THE ECONOMIST, October 26, 2013, p. 56. Foreign election observers noted "breaches and irregularities... enough to cast doubt on the election's legitimacy."

Guinea is blessed with natural resources. It is one of the world's leading producers of aluminum ore in addition to large deposits of iron, gold, and diamonds. But despite these riches "decades of dictatorship and misgovernment... have done little for ordinary Guineans, 60 percent of whom, according to UN reports, live in dire poverty." *Ibid.*

Across the Atlantic the First Nations (Indians) of Canada claim a long history of neglect and abuse. "The British depended on them in the war of 1812 against the United States but betrayed them in the peace settlement." THE ECONOMIST, October 19, 2013, p. 42.

Colonial powers took away most of the Indians' land. Then Canadian governments continued doing the same by "treaty or trickery and forced their children into residential schools aimed at assimilation." But assimilation failed regardless of the reason(s).

At the residential schools the children faced "grisly punishments—a needle through the tongue or electric shocks—for speaking their mother tongue." *Ibid.* To top it off, many students were sexually abused.

Recent Canadian governments are trying to make amends for past wrongs by apologizing and paying "almost four billion Canadian dollars to 80,000 victims of those now-closed residential schools." *Ibid.*

Shawn Atleo, speaking for Canada's 633 Indian bands, says that a "First Nationer is more likely to go to jail than graduate from high school. The graduation rate for First Nations' youth... is 36%," about half that of the rest of the country.

Abuse of school children is not restricted to a certain country or social status. The authority invested in a teacher over students is not always sacred.

Horace Mann is an elite school in New York City. As Caitlin Flanagan writes, "The culture inside and outside of Horace Mann in the 1970s allowed sexual abuse to go unchecked." THE ATLANTIC, January/February 2016, pp. 40-42.

In the 1970s there was an "absence of cultural vigilance regarding sex between teachers and students" that preceded what is called the "sexual and personal liberation of the American teenager." *Ibid.* Both phenomena challenged the existing social norms and suggested that teenagers might form "egalitarian relationships with adult figures of authority, including even teachers."

In 2012 the scandal about the Horace Mann school erupted. Amos Kamil, a journalist, published a NEW YORK TIMES MAGAZINE essay titled "Prep-School Predators" about the "widespread practices of sexual abuse" at the elite school from the late 1960s to the early 1990s.

Kamil, an alumnus of the school, first heard about the abuse while on a camping trip with four other alumni in the early 1990s. One of them confessed that the football coach, a legendary and beloved figure at the school, "raped him when he was in the eighth grade." Three of Kamil's four friends told "horrifying stories of sexual assault by teachers at the school."

For years Kamil kept this information to himself. Then in 2011 the Jerry Sandusky scandal at Pennsylvania State University broke and reminded the journalist of the Horace Mann school.

> The combination of the horrific stories and the happy-go-lucky man accused of being a rapist—a rapist charged with the task of taking care of defenseless children—was deeply disturbing. And it made me think of Horace Mann.

The elite school in New York City was not an isolated case. Almost concurrently, scandals were disclosed about the Boy Scouts as well as in the Catholic Church.

Finally there was an end to the era of keeping sexual abuse—especially the abuse of boys by men—a shameful, life-long secret.

A year after Amos Kamil's essay was published, Marc Fisher, a reporter and another Horace Mann alumnus, wrote an essay in THE NEW YORKER about "The Master," who was "one of the school's most notorious alleged abusers."

Ultimately the scandal resulted in credible charges of abuse against 22 teachers.

Over the past several years female teachers in different schools went to trial for raping male students. The unfamiliar, new trend did not go unnoticed by Hollywood which produced a movie about a sexual relationship where a female teacher seduced one of her students.

Grown-ups in Central and South America suffer from gang violence that overflows to cover a whole nation or nations.

Oscar Martinez, a Salvadoran journalist, describes the agony and fear that hapless Guatemalans, Hondurans, and Salvadorans feel in their homelands. In Central America "men and women are executed by gangs for reasons no one can understand, forcing those around them to flee for their lives to the one place they think they can be safe, the United States." THE ECONOMIST, October 26, 2013, p. 94.

In his book THE BEAST: RIDING THE RAILS AND DODGING NARCOS ON THE MIGRANT TRAIL, Martinez describes his first-hand experience during eight trips "huddled with migrants on the roof of La Bestia (The Beast), [as] the train takes them from southern to northern Mexico on the way to America, threatening at any moment to grind them with its steel wheels if they lose their frozen grip on the hand-holds."

Along their horrendous way to freedom some migrants are "shot dead and thrown off boxcars" when the armed gangsters discover whatever little bundles of money they have hidden on them.

How cruel *man* can be when he is in a position of power and control with no accountability to anyone.

In the 21st century one can hardly imagine that slavery is still flourishing. The deep-rooted practice has been known to humanity since Biblical times.

The Renaissance, the period from the 14th to the 17th century, and then the Enlightenment of the 18th century have left their mark on the spiritual and philosophical thinking of the European citizenry. The Industrial Revolution of the 19th century altered the social fabric of European and American society. Families spread apart in search of industrial jobs that commonly existed in big cities making them even bigger. The Emancipation Proclamation issued by President Abraham Lincoln on January 1, 1863 ended the institution of slavery in the United Sates.

But if you think slavery had vanished from the world stage, you are in for a surprise.

Walk Free is a foundation based in Australia and supported by philanthropists like the mining magnate Andrew Forrest. It defines slavery to include "coerced work (including the provision for sex) and children forced into marriage," THE ECONOMIST, October 19, 2013, p. 66. In 2013 the campaign published the first Global Slavery Index to include the world's 30 million slaves in 162 countries.

According to the Walk Free report, only 10 countries have 75 percent (22.5 million) of the slaves. Mauritania, a Northwest African nation, comes out worst, with "an estimated four percent of the population enslaved." Most of them are born into slavery.

India has 14 million people (or 1.129 percent) born into slavery. For 40 years India has had laws on the books that criminalize this hateful practice but the laws are "poorly enforced."

Pakistan has 1.187 percent of its population enslaved. This translates into about 2.24 million people.

As percentages, these figures may seem low, but as absolute numbers, the figures are staggering.

China has 0.218 percent of its 1.371 billion people enslaved, which amounts to about three million people.

"Europe's slavery rates are the lowest, but even in Britain, one of the lowest-ranked countries, the survey reckons up to 4,600 people are enslaved." *Ibid.* These include women engaged in prostitution and people with mental or family problems who are coerced into working.

A few years after the 2013 Walk Free report was published, THE WALL STREET JOURNAL had an editorial titled "Ending Modern Slavery," June 11-12, 2016, p. A12. The article is based on the 2016 Global Slavery Index report by the same foundation. The 2016 report index was compiled using a "rigorous methodology involving in-person interviews with 42,000 respondents in 53 languages and 25 countries."

Regrettably, the 30 million slaves noted in the 2013 report turned out to be 45.8 million in 2016. Whether the 50 percent increase is due to a more sophisticated approach of counting or is due to more oppression is unclear.

Modern-day slaves cover the gamut from North Koreans "toiling in Kim Jong Un's vast gulag," to Yazidi girls captured in Iraq by ISIS for sex slavery, to Burmese men working on "Thai shrimp boats and punished by stingray tails." *Ibid.*

The road to slavery varies by country and region, but dictatorship and slavery go hand in hand.

Percentage-wise, the 2016 Global Slavery Index has North Korea at the top with 4.373 percent of its population classified as slaves. Uzbekistan has 3.973 percent, Cambodia 1.648 percent, India has 1.403 percent while each of Qatar, Pakistan, Sudan, Iraq, and Afghanistan has 1.13 percent of its population as slaves (the last five are Muslim-majority countries with oppressive practices against women).

Looking at absolute numbers of slaves, India is at the top with 18.4 million, followed by Pakistan (2.1 million), Uzbekistan (1.2 million), North Korea (1.1 million), Congo (873,100), Sudan (454,700), Iraq (403,800), Afghanistan (367,000), Cambodia (256,800), and Qatar (30,000).

According to the 2016 Global Slavery Index, India, China, and Pakistan have more than half of all enslaved persons worldwide.

In the United States the foundation estimates that there are some 58,000 slaves (0.018 percent). Many of them are Latino illegal immigrants "who fall victim to human traffickers." Some are domestic workers who arrive legally but end up enslaved by greedy employers while others get trapped into the sex trade.

The American government and business leaders are taking aim at the practice by blocking imported goods made by slaves. The Walk Free Foundation calls on firms to "answer the abolitionist call." *Ibid.*

CHAPTER 16

OVER THE WORLD

A few years ago Europe commemorated the centenary of the First World War. From 1914 to 1918 "perhaps 8.5 million people died… but more than one million of these were from the British empire," writes Ann Wroe, obituaries editor of THE ECONOMIST, "THE WORLD IN 2014," pp. 83-84.

In British history only one war is called "Great."

Wroe wonders why the Britons gave WWI that name. The death toll of 8.5 million people was considerably less than the 60 million who perished in WWII that lasted for six years from 1939 to 1945. Also the Second World War "sprawled to the Asia-Pacific theater," whereas most of the First War was "confined to one small, clayey corner of France and Belgium." The four-year duration of WWI does not qualify it as "Great" especially if compared to the Hundred Years' War that "spanned the 14th and 15th centuries." *Ibid.*

Wroe believes that the title "Great" sprang perhaps from the strategic disaster of the battle of the Somme which had seen the loss of "more than five percent of the force on one day, July 1, 1916."

There was nothing great about WWI nor about any other war. There was only misery brought upon the world as the "inevitable outcome of itching rivalries between the great powers of the time." *Ibid.*

Soldiers were conscripted in the thousands and sent to their deaths by "decorated generals well away from the lines, but such has been the lot of soldiers" since wars began.

Bloody clashes dot world history. At some point a great power feels justified in expanding its territory to bring more resources under its control. The appetite for dominance and conquering goes unchecked until external or internal forces start to halt the momentum.

Sometimes conflict emerges between neighboring countries. Ethnic or religious disparities ignite and reignite old flames into years of war.

"A European looking forward into 1914 could easily have imagined renewed fighting in the Balkans," writes Robert Cottrell. THE ECONOMIST, "THE WORLD IN 2014," pp. 84-85.

Even though the Balkan Wars went on during 1912 and 1913, no one expected this "local kindling to turn all of Europe into a bonfire." Even Britain had to jump in.

Some argued that the great powers of Europe were heavily arming themselves and "lending lesser countries the money to do likewise." This was considered economic foolishness rather than strategic policy.

Cottrell believes that the European powers were "playing a double game, of which their proxy battles in the Balkans were a part." Whereas they sought peace and prosperity in Europe, they "also wanted to preserve or (in Germany's case) establish their own dominance within it."

The aggression of *man* or of a nation appears to be an intrinsic human impulse with the potential for bringing widespread destruction and misery.

But the danger escaped many. Western European citizens believed that their leaders would not let the situation get out of control. The European powers had "contained the first and second Balkan conflicts," and they could do the same again if the situation called for it.

In 1914 Britons expected trouble in Ireland—not in the Balkans. The Protestants of Belfast and the surrounding countries were active in opposing "home rule, and with it the transfer of powers from London to a parliament in Dublin." *Ibid.*

In America attention was focused on the Revolutionary War in Mexico next door, as well as on Panama where the American-built canal was to be opened in 1914.

Ann Wroe writes that people attributed the distinction between World War I and other wars to the "brutal disconnection between the way the war was welcomed in 1914... and the awful disillusion as it bogged down and the casualties mounted." *Ibid.*

Optimism is challenged by reality.

> The Great War came to signify lives wasted to no purpose; in that, it had no rivals... This was the war after which there were meant to be no more; each subsequent war [and there were many], therefore, was a betrayal of those who died in it, a sign that the world had not, after all, honored their sacrifice. *Ibid.*

Cottrell concludes his article with a quote that appeared in the 1913 closing issue of <u>THE SPECTATOR</u>. "One great advantage of the present time, which is the outcome of many past disadvantages and much tribulation, is that men have had their fill of fighting."

The sad yet optimistic tone conveyed more than a hundred years ago sheds light on *man's* continued tendency for aggression and control.

It has been reported that the 20th century went down in history as the bloodiest. Wishful thinking that WWI was "the war after which there were meant to be no more," looks like a mirage that is as old as creation itself when Cain killed his only brother, at the time, Abel.

A milder form of war is protesting. Laza Kekic writes, "From anti-austerity movements to middle-class revolts, in rich countries and poor, social unrest has been on the rise around the world." THE ECONOMIST, "THE WORLD IN 2014," p. 80.

"THE ECONOMIST INTELLIGENCE UNIT" (EIU) measures the risk of social unrest in 150 countries spread around the world. Different reasons cause protests. Economic distress is a major factor. Revolting against a dictatorship is another reason. Aspirations of the new middle class in fast-growing emerging markets have also been reported as a source of dissatisfaction and protesting.

But all these varied reasons share some underlying features. "The common backdrop is the 2008-09 financial crisis and its aftermath." Ironically, no single person could be found responsible for the depression many believe was second only to the Great Depression of 1929-39.

A complicated scheme allowed financial institutions to sometimes extend loans to unqualified customers. These mortgages were grouped and sold to bigger banks who sliced, insured, and then resold the equities. Once overextended customers started missing their payments, the house of cards did not take long to collapse. Housing prices dropped sharply as inventory kept mounting. Many middle-class families got burned.

Whether it was customers' greed or lax lending practices by profit-hungry financial institutions, the crisis had far-reaching implications and extended to many parts of the world. Greece, Italy, and Spain saw long-lasting protests.

Although economic distress is an imperative condition for major social instability, it is by itself not a sufficient one. "Declines in income and high unemployment are not always followed by unrest," writes Kekic. *Ibid.*

Risk of instability mounts considerably when some other elements accompany economic troubles. These include "wide income-inequality, poor government, low levels of social provision, ethnic tensions, and a history of unrest." *Ibid.*

One additional factor is the declining level of trust in governments and institutions in developed nations. The trend began to be felt in the 1970s but accelerated after the collapse of the Soviet Union in 1989. Opinion polls have documented that the level of distrust has shot up again after the 2008-09 financial crisis.

The 2013 EIU's report classifies the 150 countries according to their risk of future social unrest. It predicted that 65 countries (43 percent of the 150) will be at a high or very high risk of revolt. The 2013 analysis puts 19 more countries in this high/very high risk categories than it did in 2008.

The increase in the number of the high risk group over the past few years could be associated with the spread of social media, satellite television, smartphones, and other technological tools. Governments can no longer have a monopoly over what their people hear or watch. Dissatisfaction in one country may ignite the same in another if people, consciously or subconsciously, share similar circumstances.

Middle East and North African (MENA) nations are well represented in the high risk categories. "Twelve of the 18 MENA states" are liable to major social unrest.

The same applies to the Balkan countries where six of the seven nations included in the report are likely to see rebellion in their ranks. "More than 40 percent of the countries in Eastern Europe" are in the high risk group. Many high risk countries are in sub-Saharan Africa, which comes as no surprise to a region transitioning from colonial rule to independence.

Turkey falls in the high risk group. Its location at the junction between Asia and Europe and its membership in the North Atlantic Treaty Organization (NATO) lends Turkey some geopolitical status that exceeds its regional boundaries. Disturbances in Turkey can have far-reaching implications.

"Turkish Politics: No Longer a Shining Example," is the title of an ECONOMIST article that appeared on January 4, 2014, pp. 37-38. "Governments fall in Turkey either because they are massively corrupt or because generals boot them out (or both)."

Kemal Ataturk in 1928 catapulted Turkey on a prosperous path to democracy away from the dominant Islamic culture that had prevailed for centuries when the Ottoman empire pioneered Islamic wars against the Christian West. After the end of WWI and the defeat of the Ottomans, Ataturk envisioned a better future for Turkey through the adoption of European civilization. The country enjoyed a rather democratic system of government, and Turkey pulled away from neighboring Islamic nations.

But the positive tide did not continue. In 2002 voters got fed up with the "greed and ineptitude" of the secular political parties and opted to choose Recep Tayyip Erdogan as prime minister when his "mildly Islamic Justice and Development (AK) Party" got the majority of the votes. *Ibid.*

In Turkish, AK means "white" or "pure." After a decade in power, AK has proven "not to be exceptional after all and finds itself mired in one of the biggest graft scandals in recent history." *Ibid.*

In December 2013 police arrested 50 people suspected of tender rigging, covert gold transfers to Iran and bribery charges. Among those arrested were three cabinet ministers and the general manager of the second biggest state lender, Halkbank, who had in his home $4.5 million crammed into shoe boxes.

The probe got closer to Erdogan himself as authorities ordered a second raid that "would have netted his son, who is alleged to have enriched himself through shady property deals." *Ibid.*

The prime minister's response was typical of other dictators.

He reassigned hundreds of police chiefs and sacked a prosecutor involved in the investigation. But more crucially Erdogan ordered the laws to be rewritten in ways that would "allow the government to stop corruption probes against its own." *Ibid.* His increasing authoritarian tendencies disturbed his people and further delayed ongoing negotiations on Turkey's inclusion in the European Union (EU).

On May 28, 2013 anti-government protests erupted initially to dispute a development plan for Istanbul's Taksim park.

A sit-in at the park was violently expelled. Subsequently, supporting protests and strikes took place across Turkey. Protesters had concerns about "freedom of the press, of expression, assembly, and the government's encroachment on Turkey's secularism." Three and a half million people (out of 80 million) are estimated to have taken part in almost "5,000 demonstrations across Turkey." The protests continued until August 20, 2013. *Ibid.*

Erdogan blamed "foreign mischief-makers," for the protests, with Israel and the U.S. as leaders. A thorn in Erdogan's side is a hard-nosed imam named Fethullah Gulen who resides in Pennsylvania where he runs a "global empire of schools, media outlets, and charities." *Ibid.*

The crisis is not just about a power struggle between Erdogan and Gulen. It "highlights the chronic weaknesses of Turkey's wobbly democracy: a shackled media; a politicized judiciary; a flawed, illiberal constitution; and a lack of independent scrutiny of public accounts." *Ibid.*

Here is one man, Erdogan, who uses his authority to derail years of a rare successful experiment of an Islamic country with democracy.

Could this be attributed to the Islamic tendencies of the prime minister?

Ataturk's efforts to bring democracy to a Muslim-majority Turkey worked for a few decades but apparently is losing ground to the traditional authoritarian rule that has always prevailed in Islamic societies. Many question whether democracy and Islam are compatible.

And the protests of the summer of 2013 did not end Erdogan's troubles.

In July 2016 an "alleged coup d'etat was attempted in Turkey... against the government and President Recep Tayyip Erdogan. The attempt was carried out by a faction within the Turkish Armed Forces." *Ibid.* The bloody coup attempt left more than 200 dead. It is believed that Fethullah Gulen was behind the failed attempt.

Subsequently, Erdogan's AK Party "sharpened the crackdown on its critics, starting with journalists, surpassing even China." *Ibid*. Turkey requested that the United States extradite Gulen to face charges at home. The request has been denied.

Apparently, the modern-day Turkish dictator's policies did not stand in the way of his election as president. The constitution prevents him from running for a fourth term as prime minister. The presidency fulfills his desire for power and control.

SUMMARY, CONCLUSION, AND A
BRIGHTER PERSPECTIVE

This book is an attempt to discuss the weakness of *man*. It has rightly been said that power corrupts and absolute power corrupts absolutely.

Politically, the forefathers realized the danger of power in the hands of man, so they established the doctrine of separation of powers to guarantee that no branch of the government could encroach on the other two branches.

Lately, however, the judicial branch has been overstepping its boundaries by legislating rather than interpreting the law. This seeming usurpation of power has brought dismay to many.

Michael Savage writes,

> When the Supreme Court told Americans of every state it was overturning their laws concerning gay marriage... Washington was going to decide how marriage is governed in all fifty states. It is not a matter of whether gay marriage itself is right or wrong. It's a matter of who decides. TRUMP'S WAR, HIS BATTLE FOR AMERICA, Center Street, New York, Nashville, 2017, p. 3.

Even in the well-established democratic system of the United States, *man* still can find his way towards dominance.

His job is made much easier in authoritarian regimes based entirely on the monopoly of power by a single person. To remedy the appearance of absolute control, a political party may stand behind the strongman. All authority resides within the single party and opposition is muted.

Even religion has not proved to be immune from *man's* tendency for aggression.

Rome, with the Pope at the helm, exercised what was "believed" to be good for Christianity. Those who dared to challenge the power of Rome suffered torture and persecution.

For centuries Europe endured atrocities committed in the name of Christianity. The religion of love and forgiveness was sacrificed at the altar of *man's* greed, ambition, and cruelty. Many left to escape tyranny and start a new life in what is now known as the United States.

The abuse of power by Islamic leaders and clergy is as old as Islam itself. Since its inception in the seventh century, autocratic rule has been the norm. No dissention or discussion is allowed. Islam was spread by the sword. Citizens of conquered nations had to choose between converting to Islam, paying exuberant taxes, or being beheaded.

Democracy and the rule of law have had a hard time in the Muslim world.

For a limited time, a glimmer of hope appeared in Turkish politics but is "no longer a shining example." The three-term prime minister maneuvered his way to the presidency. His Islamist and dictatorial tendencies are becoming increasingly evident.

The Creator has bestowed man with a mind to think and the freedom to choose and enjoy life within some boundaries set not to deprive man of pleasure but to keep him from destroying himself and others around him. But some choose rebellion against God, bringing misery upon themselves and, in many cases, upon others as well.

Sin entered the world with one man, Adam. Salvation and the hope of eternal life have been offered by the Son of man, the Lord Jesus Christ. The battle between good and evil continues until His second coming.

Enough of the wrongdoings committed by *man*.

The discovery of the "New World" ushered in a new era of man's history. The doors were open to those who sought a new beginning in a faraway land where they could worship freely. With faith in God and relentless hard work, a young, prosperous, and powerful nation was born.

Simon Winchester was born in England and became an American citizen in 2011. His love for his adopted homeland led him to write a book titled "THE MEN WHO UNITED THE STATES: THE AMAZING STORIES OF THE EXPLORERS, INVENTORS, AND MAVERICKS WHO MADE AMERICA." William Collins, THE ECONOMIST, January 4, 2014, p. 67.

Winchester uses stories to "paint an unusual and personal portrait of the creation of a nation." The book is divided into five sections, each one dominated by wood, earth, water, fire, or metal. Interestingly, this classification allows "chronological movement too."

Winchester begins with the "great journey... of Meriwether Lewis and William Clark in the first years of the 19th century." Many believe that this journey gave America a "vision of its own size and scope." Lewis and Clark's historic expedition reached the Pacific Ocean in November 1805. Its goals included the exploration of territory for "timber."

John Wesley Powell's "earth" exploration in the years after the Civil War led him to the Grand Canyon.

With "water" comes the Panama Canal which connects the Atlantic and Pacific Oceans. Built in the early 20th century, it cuts across the Isthmus of Panama. Its 48-mile length makes it the eighth wonder of the world. The Canal is a "key conduit for international maritime trade."

"Fire" encompasses the building of both railways and roads. By 1850 over 9,000 miles of railroad lines had been built. The First Transcontinental Railroad in the U. S. was built in the 1860s. Walt W. Rostow believes that railroads were responsible for the beginning of American industrialization in the period of 1843-1860.

"Metal" denotes the introduction of "wires—telegraph, telephone, and finally the Internet—that allow Americans to communicate daily."

> Men... battled long odds to build a great nation. Many of these names have been nearly forgotten... Winchester revives them.... Theodore Dehone Judah first envisioned a transcontinental railway, Morris Llewellyn Cooke brought electricity to America's heartland. Cal Rogers made the first transcontinental flight in 1911-12. *Ibid.*

The capacity of man to do good never vanishes. By the same token, his negative tendencies could get the best of him. The struggle between good and evil has always been and will ever be a hallmark of humanity.

Printed in the United States
By Bookmasters